AM I BEING TOO SUBTLE?

AM I BEING TOO SUBTLE?

Straight Talk from a Business Rebel

Sam Zell

Portfolio / Penguin

An imprint of Penguin Random House LLC
375 Hudson Street
New York, New York 10014

Most Portfolio books are available at a discount when purchased in quantity for sales promotions or corporate use. Special editions, which include personalized covers, excerpts, and corporate imprints, can be created when purchased in large quantities. For more information, please call (212) 572-2232 or e-mail specialmarkets@penguinrandomhouse.com. Your local bookstore can also assist with discounted bulk purchases using the Penguin Random House corporate Business-to-Business program. For assistance in locating a participating retailer, e-mail B2B@penguinrandomhouse.com.

ISBN 9781591848233 (hardcover)
ISBN 9780698408883 (e-book)

Printed in the United States of America
3   5   7   9   10   8   6   4

Book design by Amy Hill

Penguin is committed to publishing works of quality and integrity.
In that spirit, we are proud to offer this book to our readers; however,
the story, the experiences, and the words are the author's alone.

The purpose of this book is to educate and entertain. The author does not guarantee that anyone following the techniques, suggestions, tips, ideas, or strategies will become successful. The author shall have neither liability nor responsibility to anyone with respect to any loss or damage caused or alleged to be caused, directly or indirectly, by the information contained in this book.

To the immigrants who made this possible.

CONTENTS

AM I BEING TOO SUBTLE?

INTRODUCTION

No B.S.

No one has ever left a meeting with me wondering what I meant. When I say something it is clear, candid, and often blunt. "Am I being too subtle?" is my punch line when I deliver a message I consider obvious. I'll occasionally add, "I can speak slower if you want," to ensure my point is received.

I can seem gruff. I know that. And I can be impatient. I have an embedded sense of urgency. What I can't figure out is why so many other people *don't* have it. But from an early age I realized that I had a fundamentally different perspective from my peers. And I was willing to trade conformity for authenticity—even when that meant being an outlier, which it usually did, and even if it meant being on my own.

In this book I share the story of how a restless, curious boy who grew up in Chicago made it to the Forbes 400. I'll describe the risks that paid off and those that didn't—and tell you what I learned in the process. I'll take you inside my world of companies, where culture is king. That is, we take great care with the *way* we do things—with transparency, alignment, and trust.

I am probably best known for creating several of the largest companies in commercial real estate and for helping establish today's $1 trillion public real estate industry. But most of my investments are actually in other industries, like energy, manufacturing, retail, travel, logistics, health care, and so on. You could say I'm an investor, or an allocator of capital. But what I really am is an entrepreneur. I focus less on specific industries and more on seeing opportunity in anomalies or trends that catch my attention.

I also read risk for a living. I am very focused on understanding the downside. And I have a pretty good track record, but it's not perfect. You can't play at this level without some pretty big highs and lows. Of course, they don't usually happen within the same couple of years, but they did for me in 2007–2008 with our $39 billion sale of Equity Office, the company I built from scratch, and the $8 billion privatization of Tribune Company, which closed at the start of the Great Recession and went into bankruptcy a year later.

In real estate I'm known as the Grave Dancer. That was the title of an article I wrote back in 1976, and the nickname stuck. Some might see buying and creating value from others' mistakes as a form of exploitation, but I see it as giving neglected or devalued assets, in any industry, new life. And often in my career I've been the only bidder for them—the last chance for a resurrection. I'm not claiming to be altruistic—just optimistic, and confident that I can turn those assets around.

That, in my definition, is an entrepreneur. Someone who doesn't just see the problems but also sees the solutions—the opportunities.

Not surprisingly, a fundamental part of being an entrepreneur aligns with my tendency to walk out of step with the norm.

I have a saying: "If everyone is going left, look right." Conventional wisdom is nothing to me but a reference point. In fact, I believe it can be a horribly debilitating concept. It often boils down to a bunch of people yelling "Go this way!" And once the crowd gets going, it can get real loud real fast. We saw it in the stampede of commercial real estate development in the 1970s and 1980s, the dot-com craze of the 1990s, and the subprime mortgage mania of the 2000s.

I make a point of shutting out the noise—doing what makes sense to *me*. I want everyone's opinion, because there is tremendous value in being a good listener. But then I determine my own path. I look for clarity, and if something's not clear, I get more information. That could mean reading various sources of news, understanding new legislation, or meeting with someone halfway across the world. The point is, I don't make assumptions. But determining my position is the easy part.

Once I have formed my opinion, I have to trust my perspective enough to act on it. That means putting my own money behind it. My level of commitment is usually high. And I stay with my decision even when everyone is telling me I'm wrong, which happens a lot. If I had a nickel for every time I heard "Sam, you just don't understand," I'd be rich.

I believe the fundamentals of business—supply and demand, liquidity equals value, good corporate governance, and reliable partners, to name a few—apply across the board. They inform my decision making, or *what* I do, just like my philosophies guide *how* I do it.

I run my company as a meritocracy with a moral compass. And for those who raise their eyebrows at that statement—who think you can't get to the top unless you beat the crap out of everybody—you're wrong. When you're a repeat player, when your world is your business and your business is your world, it's *all* about long-term relationships. In any negotiation I believe in leaving a little bit on the table. And in any relationship I believe in sharing the stakes. I've been doing deals with many of the same people for decades because the goal is for us to all come out ahead. And many of my employees have been with me for twenty or thirty years or more because if I do well, they do well.

These long-term relationships reflect the most important lesson imparted to me by my father. He taught me simply how to *be*. He often told me that nothing was more important than a man's honor—*shem tov* in the Jewish community: a good name. Reputation is your most important asset. Everything you do, everything you say, is part of the permanent record. Your name reflects your character. No matter how successful I got, I never forgot that lesson. I've always strived to be known as a man of my word.

Not that I'm a saint. I've been married three times, and I admit that when I was younger, my career competed with my role as a husband and father, and my career often won. But I've always tried to impart the best of the lessons I learned from my parents to my kids—be grounded and pragmatic, recognize a sense of responsibility, and, of course, *shem tov*.

Today I have a better perspective, as most of us get over time. The first thing you see if you walk into my office is a twenty-seven-inch screen with scrolling photos of my wife, my kids, and my grandkids. I relish my time with each of them. My life is more balanced now, and family traditions are sacred. Among my favorites are the European trips my wife of twenty years, Helen, and I take each grandkid on as a rite of passage upon his or her sixteenth birthday. My hope is these trips encourage their curiosity in the world and help them understand their lives in a larger context. I want them to learn to form their own opinions and give them confidence to act on their convictions. These are the traits, after all, that saved the lives of my parents, sisters, and me, as you'll learn. And this perspective is the reason for much of my success.

But I am not solely, or even primarily, motivated by the accumulation of wealth. There's a line from an old movie, *Wheeler Dealers*: "You don't go wheeling and dealing for the money, you do it for fun. Money's just a way of keeping score." And that's how I see it. I've always been much more drawn to the *experience*.

My life is about testing my limits—and having fun in the process. I believe that 1 + 1 can equal 3. Or 4. Or 6. The fun and gratification are in figuring out how. For me, business is not a battle to be waged—it's a puzzle to be solved. And the end goal isn't to accumulate a lot of toys and then kick back. Since I was a twelve-year-old who spent afternoons exploring the streets of Chicago alone, I've been hungry for new experiences. So I've never understood the traditionally strict boundary between "work" and "fun." If I'm being intellectually challenged, if I'm doing things I've never done before, if I'm using my creativity and resources to solve problems, if I'm constantly learning—*that* is fun.

There's a healthy amount of irreverence at my core, and I apply it in an equal-opportunity way—externally and internally. Early on I adopted a philosophy I call the Eleventh Commandment, "Thou shalt not take thyself too seriously," and it became a governing principle in my life. Big investment deals can get heady at times, and it can be easy to start thinking your brand is bigger than your performance. I never want that to be me.

And hopefully it's contagious. Back in 1985, the *Wall Street Journal* did a front-page story on me and quoted me saying "If it ain't fun, we don't do it." The next day I walked into the office and all the mailroom guys were wearing T-shirts with that quote. I loved the fact that they thought to do it, that they felt they could, and that they made it happen. That epitomizes the culture at my investment firm, Equity Group Investments (EGI).

One of the biggest raps about me is that I've been known to use profanity. Sure, sometimes my real estate colleagues will make over/under bets on whether or when I'll drop the f-bomb onstage at a conference. I simply don't buy into many of the made-up rules of social convention. I think people often get distracted by these superficialities. For example, I've been wearing jeans to work since the 1960s, long before it was acceptable. And to this day, I'm usually the only one at a business conference or on CNBC's *Squawk Box* set in jeans. The bottom line is if you're really good at what you do, you have the freedom to be who you really are.

I am the son of Jewish immigrants who fled Poland to escape the Holocaust and come to the United States. My entire life is dedicated to the idea that I am part of the great American dream, an entrepreneurial movement like none other in the world. What I want to do is use my gifts to find opportunities no one else sees, solve problems others can't, do great deals, turn around broken assets, and grow great companies. In short, I want to make a difference. I don't mean that in a pious way. I'm talking about *progress*—shaking up the status quo, moving the needle, building something meaningful. And always treading where others aren't. Some of my most interesting and lucrative investments seemed counterintuitive when I made them—such as buying rail cars when the industry was crumbling, or investing in manufactured home communities when other investors wouldn't touch them.

People often ask me, "When are you going to retire?" And I answer, "Retire from what?" I've never worked a day in my life.

Everything I've done has been because I've loved doing it, because it was enthralling. I thrive on inspiring and challenging people, giving them new opportunities and watching them grow, and I take enormous pride in their accomplishments. And I never stop pushing—myself or others. I'm seventy-five; I work out every morning at 4:45, I'm at the office by 6:30 a.m., and I don't get home from work until 7:00 at night.

I have plenty more to do and a lot more to say. Every day is an adventure.

Here's my story. Have fun with it.

CHAPTER ONE

An Impossible Life

My father was the first person I knew who had done something "impossible." At thirty-four, he escaped his hometown in Poland on the last train out, just hours before the Luftwaffe bombed the tracks, and then led my mother and two-year-old sister on a twenty-one-month trek across two continents to safety.

As a result, I grew up believing that anything is possible. And when you're not aware there are any limitations, nothing stops you from trying.

My parents each grew up in middle-class homes in Polish towns close to the German border. They were from large families, both of which were devoutly Jewish and highly educated. They were distant cousins and met through family, and after they married in 1936 they stayed in the region, settling in a town called Sosnowiec.

My father, Bernard, bought and sold grain throughout Eastern Europe. By virtue of traveling to different countries and interfacing with different people and cultures, he had a more worldly perspective and was more attuned to geopolitics than most of his family and neighbors. He was also an avid follower of current events and relied on his shortwave radio for news, since radio in Poland was censored. He and my mother listened to reports in different languages, including reports from Germany, Britain, and America. So he was very aware of the growing danger for Jews in Poland at a time when many of his more provincial friends and family dismissed the possibility of extreme scenarios.

My father was a realist, and a man of foresight and action. By 1937, growing anti-Semitism in Poland, and Germany's increasing aggression, concerned him enough to take action. My mother, Rochelle, sewed jewelry into the lining of some of their clothes to use as currency in case they had to escape, but they knew they would need more funds than they could carry. At the time, Poland had outlawed the transfer of assets out of the country, and people suspected of economic crimes were known to disappear. So my father took an enormous risk by making a clandestine transfer of money to a bank in Tel Aviv (then Palestine). To avoid detection, he requested that no confirmation of the deposit be sent.

A year later, by the time of the Kristallnacht in late 1938, my father had made the final decision to leave. But he first wanted to establish a broader economic base outside of Poland. The plan was to confirm that the funds he had sent to the Anglo-Palestine Bank in Palestine were indeed there, send those funds to a bank in the U.S. and replace them with more money from Poland. This money transfer operation was organized by a Jewish agency to help Jews move their assets out of Poland. To make the transfers, however, my father needed my mother's help, and they had to be very careful.

He went to Tel Aviv on a three-week tourist visa, and wrote my mother every day to make his communications back home seem commonplace. Every letter coming in or going out of Poland was read by police, so he had to provide inconspicuous clues as to what he needed her to do. Each of his letters emphasized the number "50," which my mother knew indicated she was to prepare 50,000 zlotys (about $10,000). (They kept all their money that was in Poland in the house.) One day, my mother received the typical envelope, but all that fell out was a tiny piece of torn paper with just a few words on it. It was odd, and she knew it meant something but had no idea what. Then, on the last week of my father's trip, a stranger showed up, unannounced, on the family's doorstep. This was in itself always an anxiety-producing event. The man said he was the president of the Anglo-Palestine Bank, and he had a carbon copy of the little torn piece of paper my mother had received in the mail from my father, so she gave the stranger the 50,000 zlotys. He could have been from the police or he could have just kept the money. She had no real way of knowing how genuine he was. But it all worked out; my father returned home having completed his mission. He had added money to his account in Tel Aviv and transferred money to a bank in New York, listing both his and Rochelle's signatures on the accounts.

My parents each had six siblings, and they made numerous appeals to their brothers, sisters, and parents to leave Poland. But every one of their family members refused to consider it. Like many people in the community, in spite of witnessing and experiencing anti-Semitism, they thought they would be okay if they just stuck it out, like they had during the Great War. After all, the Germans were civilized, cultured people. Certainly the prospect of leaving their entire families behind delayed my father's decision to pull the trigger.

Then, on August 24, 1939, my father was traveling east on a business trip to Warsaw when his train made a stop at the halfway point. He saw a newsboy selling papers and stepped off to buy one. The headline read that Germany and the Soviet Union had just signed a nonaggression pact. He knew with certainty that Poland, squeezed in the middle between Germany and Russia, would be attacked from both sides and divided between the two aggressors. It was time to get out. My father immediately crossed the tracks to board a train heading back home.

His train arrived in Sosnowiec at 2:00 p.m. It was a ten-minute walk home, and when he got there he told my mother to pack what she could carry; they were boarding the 4:00 train out that afternoon.

He took my mother and sister Julie to a relative's house in Kielce, about seventy-five miles away, and then returned to their hometown in one last effort to beg their families to leave Poland with them. It felt like a race against time. But again they refused. So my parents and sister started out alone on a nearly two-year odyssey. The Germans invaded Poland at dawn. My father had caught the last train out of Sosnowiec before the Nazis bombed the railroad tracks.

My family couldn't go west toward Germany, so they headed northeast, across Poland, into Lithuania. They traveled on foot, by bus, by horse-drawn carts, and by cattle train. They were often part of an early wave of refugees to enter each city. Growing up, I heard many stories of the help my family received along the way—often from my father's business associates, Jews and non-Jews alike. For that reason he always impressed upon us the importance of *tzedakah*—righteousness, kindness, and giving to others. *Tzedakah* saved my parents' lives.

In Vilnius, Lithuania, they rested and my father began selling grain to local merchants. My mother was tired of running and wanted to settle there to wait out the war. But my father never lost his sense of urgency to get out. He was right, of course. Most of the Jews who remained in Lithuania perished.

His ultimate goal was either Palestine or the U. S., but first they had to get out of Europe, and for that they needed visas from a safe country that was willing to accept them. There were few consulates left in Vilnius, and most were from countries in Western Europe that were already at war or under German occupation. However, there was an honorary Dutch consul named Jan Zwartendijk who lived in nearby Kaunas, and the Dutch-controlled island of Curaçao, off the coast of Venezuela, didn't require visas to get in. The bad news was that the Dutch government literally didn't have a process to issue visas for Curaçao; no such visa existed, and the refugees needed something official-looking to travel through the Soviet Union. So a Jewish tradesman in the refugee group crafted a fake stamp with the Dutch crest and brought it to Zwartendijk, who then used it to forge entrance visas for Curaçao.

The island was located fifty-six hundred miles southwest of Lithuania, on the far side of Poland, Germany, and France. Clearly, travel through those countries was not an option. The only way to Curaçao was through Russia and Japan, a journey of eight thousand miles, across the entire continent, to then go west. An additional hurdle was the necessity of a travel visa for Japan.

A Jewish refugee delegation, including my father, went to the Vilnius Japanese vice consul, Chiune Sugihara, for these transit visas. Sugihara wired Tokyo three times for permission to help the refugees, but was denied each time. The vice consul was a Japanese career diplomat, but he had also been raised in a middle-class samurai family. And part of the code of the samurai is benevolence and mercy, and appreciation and respect for life. Despite the risk to his career and his family, Sugihara ignored his direct orders and decided to do as much as he could.

For the next month, he and his wife barely stopped to eat or sleep as they wrote out thousands of transit visas. My family was among the six thousand Jews Sugihara saved—the Sugihara Survivors.

It's always been remarkable to me that my parents' lives were saved by a Japanese man disobeying orders, considering the Japanese culture. When I went to Japan for the first time in the early 1980s and told this story to the people I was meeting, they flat out said it couldn't be true—an official in the Foreign Service would never violate a direct order. But he had. It wasn't until 1985, when Sugihara was an old man, that his actions were officially recognized in Israel. He was revered as "the Japanese Schindler" and received Israel's recognition as a Righteous Gentile by the Yad Vashem, the Holocaust Martyrs' and Heroes' Remembrance Authority.

Before Sugihara's death, we found out where he was living, and my sister Julie and her husband went to Japan to meet with him. Julie asked him, "How could you have taken that chance, against orders?" His answer was "I'd never had an opportunity to literally save people before—and then I did. And I had to do it." His courageous act became his legacy—his way to make a difference.

My parents and sister traveled across the Soviet Union on the Trans-Siberian Railway. Through every one of the fifty-six hundred miles they were at risk. Jews were being sent to camps in Siberia for any infraction, real or not, at the time, and my family was traveling in the dead of winter. But they made it; they were the second group of what would become thousands of Jewish refugees to reach Japan during the war.

My family spent nearly four months in Japan, most of it in Yokohama. My mother spoke fondly of the kindness and warmth of the Japanese people; it was meaningful, particularly after their harrowing trip. Later, after my parents had settled in the States, they struggled to reconcile their experience there with Japan's actions during the war and with their new country's animosity toward the Japanese people.

My family traveled thousands of miles, through four countries, over the course of twenty-one months to safety, arriving in Seattle on May 18, 1941. My mother was pregnant with me at the time. They had spent almost everything they had except for about $600 they had sent ahead to the Manufacturers Trust Company bank in New York.

The evening after they landed, my parents took their first English class; they were eager to improve their language skills and to begin the process of becoming Americans. My father's great-uncle in New York offered him a job, but my father was independent-minded and saw Chicago as a natural place to settle, as it was the center of the country's grain business and he expected to pick up his profession as a grain merchant.

The first hotel my parents went to in Chicago turned them away. My father was furious. His immediate reaction was "Here I thought we had finally escaped anti-Semitism. But I come to the United States, try to check in to a hotel, and they won't take us." When he'd tell the story, it was a rare moment of levity for him because it was a joke. My father couldn't read English at the time, and apparently the sign outside the hotel had read "Men Only."

My parents settled in a largely Jewish neighborhood on the West Side of Chicago. That's where I was born, on September 28, four months after my family arrived in the U.S. and two months before Pearl Harbor.

Among the last letters from my parents' families in Poland was one that told them my mother's brother-in-law, Samuel Moses, had been shot in the street. (I was subsequently named after him.) Before long their families disappeared into the ghettos, and then into the concentration camps. Most all of the family was murdered—their parents, all but two of their brothers and sisters, and all of their siblings' eighteen children. Only my mother's brother Isaac and her sister Ann survived.

My parents' worldview was cast in their survivor experience. And the imprint of the immigrant was never far from the surface in our home, even after the war ended when I was four. But I was largely ignorant of the family story until I stumbled upon it at the age of six. My parents belonged to an organization called the Harmony Circle Club, which included a bunch of Polish refugees who met once a month to share news of the war in Europe and discuss how their lives were going in America.

I vividly remember the night I snuck out of my bedroom and into the dark living room where an 8-mm film was flickering on the wall. My parents and their friends were watching a clandestine film from the concentration camps. I saw jumpy black-and-white images of trucks overflowing with bodies, bones protruding from skin, human beings discarded like garbage—absolutely horrible stuff. Those unforgettable images were my introduction to the Holocaust. Looking back, I can see that they accelerated my maturity and gave me a sober awareness of the world. That film also went a long way toward helping me understand my parents' orientation toward life—why they pushed so hard and were so determined for their children to succeed. Economic success had been critical in securing their freedom. They had escaped Poland in part because they had the means to do so—my father's prescience in storing away money.

The day after my father died in 1986, my mother gave me his pinky ring. It held the diamond they had hidden in my sister

Julie's shoe during their long escape from Europe. I transferred the stone to a bracelet that I wear on my right wrist and never take off—to always remember where I come from.

My parents imbued Julie, me and our younger sister, Leah, with their passionate and enduring gratitude for the United States. Every year for the rest of their lives, they celebrated the date of their arrival with a toast to America. My sisters and I grew up keenly aware of how fortunate we were to be in this country, where opportunity was not defined by birth or religion or anything other than drive, and where there were no limits on how much you could achieve or how far you could go.

My father was ambitious and a natural entrepreneur, but he struggled to re-create the successful career he had as a grain merchant in Poland. Quaker Oats had been one of his biggest customers back home, and his contact there had repeatedly said to him, "If only we had people of your skill level and work ethic at Quaker Oats!" So, the company was his first stop in looking for a job when he got to Chicago, but he was turned away because he didn't have a college degree.

Within two years of arriving in Chicago, my father left the grain business and started his own wholesale jewelry company. His great-uncle helped him buy a large quantity of surplus jewelry, which he then resold around the Midwest. My father was a great believer in productivity. He worked six days a week, at least thirteen hours a day. His business took him to eleven states. For him the key to business was access—getting the goods into the stores. Even with his heavy accent, my father gained access to major retailers that others had failed to sign. People responded to his confidence, his work ethic and his intelligence.

He built up his business conservatively. Prudence was his mantra; he was always deeply respectful of risk. Beneath his love of America was a lingering fear that disaster could come and grab him by the throat in the middle of the night. In essence, my father comprised a refugee's unique paradox of optimism tainted by worry. His attitude could be described as "on the one hand, go forward . . . on the other hand, hold back."

During that time, my father served as a patriarch of sorts to a large number of friends, acquaintances and business associates who came from disparate groups and backgrounds. They sought his advice and judgment because he asked smart questions, genuinely listened to the answers, and gave measured, unbiased, candid responses. The respect he generated, the way it mattered to people, and the positive impact he made in their lives made an enormous impression on me.

Today, I try to serve in that role for people, including my employees and executives, sure, but also for my kids and grandkids. Taking a long walk with one of them to talk through a problem they're having—applying that gift of Socratic dialogue my father gave me—is as rewarding as any multimillion-dollar deal.

My family sponsored and hosted a steady stream of Polish Jewish refugees when I was a kid. For several years I had to share my bedroom with men who stayed with us. I didn't think that was odd at all, but I can't imagine it would go down so well today. Imagine asking your child to give up half his room to a stranger! But it was a reflection of the time and my parents' commitment to helping others.

My parents were very disciplined and very focused on work and achievement, and they led by example. As kids our priorities were education, religion, and being a mensch—someone with integrity and honor. Certainly by today's standards they were not doting, especially my father. They were not of the generation or the culture to coddle their kids, overpraise them, or ease up to let them win. From an early age, I enjoyed competing with my father, like most boys do, I think. He took it seriously—never gave me a break as some dads would. For example, my father was a master chess player; he taught me and I became an accomplished player. One day I tried to stump him by arranging a whole scenario on the chessboard, where there was just one move to checkmate. I waited impatiently for him to come home and then proudly showed him the board. "Dad, look," I said, "I set up the board. See if you can figure out what the one move is." He looked, shrugged, made the move and walked out of the room. I was crushed. He didn't make anything easier or softer. That just wasn't who he was.

I always joke that my father made a life-and-death decision to leave Poland when he was thirty-four, and he was never wrong after that. He was very strong-willed and authoritarian, and because I had a strong personality as well, we often clashed. He continually attempted to rein me in; I always bristled at being told no. Consequently, we had a rather contentious relationship.

But I had enormous respect for my father, and that respect was absolute. He would say, "You don't have to love me, but you do have to respect me." I took that directive literally, figuring that if I didn't open my mouth to talk back, I wasn't being disrespectful and could retain an ounce of dignity. So when we disagreed, I simply clammed up and refused to speak to him. We sometimes spent months not talking to each other. It made for some very long family dinners, and my mother hated it. One time our silence lasted for three months. I don't recall what the disputes were about—who cares? We had a lot of them. The bottom line was, if I was angry, I deferred. I wouldn't take him on.

That was the respect he demanded. Ultimately, I always ended up apologizing, prompted by my mother. She would pull me aside and say, "Sammy, you can't do this." I'd respond, "Mother, he's wrong." And she'd say, "You don't understand, Sammy. He's your father, therefore he's never wrong."

Many years later, in the 1970s, my father and I would go together to the annual dinner for the Jewish Federation—which I referred to as "the big Jew dinner." It was a fund-raiser, attended by the most prominent Jews in the city. Every year my father gave a substantial donation, and I donated accordingly, less than my father. By 1979 I was successful enough to up my pledge to more than he was giving. But I couldn't do that unless I cleared it with him first. So I told him, "I'd like to make the following pledge, but I won't do it if you think that it shows a lack of *kavod*" (respect). He said, "No, no. That's wonderful," and so I did it. I was giving him respect, but he was letting me know that he respected me too. I think that was a turning point for us.

Nevertheless our similar temperaments often caused friction, and when I was a kid, this was amplified by the generational schism between us and by the conflicting values of the old and new worlds. I was their first child born in the United States. My younger sister, Leah, was born here in 1949. Our frame of reference was dramatically different than that of our parents. They constantly worried that their children would lose the traditional values that meant so much to them. They wanted us to live good lives and most of all to be good Jews. And while they loved this country, they believed that there were dangers inherent in American affluence and freedom. They felt we lacked discipline and spent too much time in pursuit of frivolous activities like sports. To my father, sports were just something that got in the way of work or study. They had no value. As a teenager, if I wanted to go to a basketball game on a Saturday night, my father's reaction would be "You went last week. Why do you need to go to another basketball game?" I would say, "Because it's fun," and he'd reply, "You have plenty of time in your life for fun. Now you have to focus. You have to achieve. You have to be directed. You've got to understand the world is a hard place." That was a typical conversation.

I remember an incident when my sister Julie was in high school. She was about fourteen, and she went to a school called Von Steuben. One afternoon, after Von Steuben had lost a big basketball game, Julie came home from school crying over her team's defeat. My parents were completely beside themselves; they didn't know what to do. They just couldn't conceive that she was crying because of a high school basketball game. It was a totally foreign concept.

I believe that the unwavering delineation my father drew between achievement and fun led me to go the exact opposite way, so that later I built my world around blending one into the other.

Our home was traditional and sober in nature, but it had great warmth. We ate dinner as a family every night, and from as early as I can remember, we would discuss world affairs, politics, and current events in the country. My parents never dumbed down the conversation for the kids. It was an environment of metaphors, a Talmudic approach, where lessons were always given from examples or stories. To this day I tell stories as a primary way of getting my point across.

My parents were very strong, very smart, and, understandably, slightly paranoid people. My father was, without question, the patriarch, and my mother was traditionally deferential. It was simply a function of the era in which they were raised. In public, my mother never disagreed with my father. For many years, I mistook her submissive role as weakness. I remember riding in a car with my father one day as he lectured me on how strong my mother really was; that even though it appeared she was the weaker of the two, the reverse was the case in many respects.

I didn't fully appreciate my mother's strength and resilience until after my father's death in 1986 when she was seventy-five. At forty-five, I was now the patriarch, which I took to mean that my mother's care was in my hands. I called her every day from wherever I was in the world, and I could always tell from her voice how she was really doing, and if it wasn't well, I knew to keep asking until she relented and spilled the problem. She and I grew much closer after we lost my father.

For that first year after my father's passing, my mother didn't go out of the house. On the day of my father's Yahrzeit, the anniversary of his death, she called me to say she was finished with her year of mourning and was ready to try something new. So I moved her from the suburbs to a penthouse on Astor Street. She became an active urbanite, and she never looked back. Before I knew it, she was making friends in the building, going to the opera and to movies and out to dinners—all things she never did while my father was alive.

She opened up to a new life, but my mother was still austere; she didn't cajole or complain to make a point. She had a steely resolve, and often said more with her actions than her words. When she wanted me to do something she'd call and the conversation would go something like this:

"Hi, Mother," I'd say.

"Sammy, David's son's bris is next Thursday."

"I know," I'd say, "but I'm scheduled to be out of town that day."

"Sammy, David's son's bris is next Thursday."

22

"I know," I'd repeat. "But I've got an appointment out of town."

"Sammy, David's son's bris is next Thursday."

Sigh. "I'll be there."

Her core values also never changed, including her frugality. My mother had a high sensitivity to waste and excess spending. My sisters and I were always taught to question value and whether something new was necessary. This frugality was imprinted on my mother to the point that even when my family became quite prosperous, her cash register mentality never went above $100.

One evening after dinner at my apartment, I offered to drive her home. She declined, no reason offered.

"Well then, I'll call a cab for you."

"No, no," she said, "I have to go to Walgreens," which was on the corner.

So, I said fine, and she went to Walgreens.

Then the next week she came for dinner and we went through the same scenario.

"Mom, I'll drive you home."

"No."

"Then I'll get you a cab."

"No, I have to go to Walgreens."

Well, the third time this happened, I followed her and saw her getting on a bus outside Walgreens. Apparently, she didn't want to put me out, and she just couldn't stand the thought of spending $3 on a taxi when for 50 cents she could use her senior discount and take the bus home. She lived half a block from the bus stop and could just walk from there. For her, it was all about the value of a dollar. A refugee never forgets.

Another time at dinner, she asked my sister Leah how much

an outfit she was wearing cost. When Leah told her it was about a thousand dollars, my mother went nuts. Just the idea of spending that kind of money on *clothes* was out of the question. Both of my sisters are very sophisticated and dress very well, and our mother's excessive frugality drove them crazy. So of course they stopped telling our mother the price of things.

As an aside, I certainly don't claim to be frugal, but my mother's sensibilities have never left me. My son-in-law tells a story about one of the first times we met. We were standing outside a grocery store waiting for my wife and daughter—his fiancée at the time. We got bored so we started looking at sunglasses at a little shop. I tried a pair on and they really fit, and we both agreed they looked good. Apparently, when I looked at the price tag, I recoiled in horror and put them back on the shelf, saying, "Two hundred dollars for *sunglasses*? Are you kidding me?"

My parents' experience dramatically shaped our home life and provided me with a different perspective than my friends'. I can still remember the moment it struck me that I wasn't like the other kids in an essential way: I was eight years old, walking home from synagogue on a Saturday. I couldn't have articulated it then, but looking back I recognize that I had a bigger-picture orientation, felt an acute sense of responsibility, and was certain my brain was my most powerful asset.

Whenever my friends and I played, I defaulted to using strategy. Of course I didn't know that's what it was at the time. When we played cops and robbers, or war, or whatever, instead of running headlong into the battle when someone yelled, "Charge!" I'd hold back and create a diversion, slip around behind someone, and surprise him. For me, the fun was being unpredictable and turning the game into an intellectual challenge.

I have an insatiable curiosity, and as a kid I thrived on wandering around my Chicago neighborhood on my own. I felt *born* to live in the city. I was eleven when my family moved to the comfortable upper-middle-class northern suburb of Highland Park. It was a hard transition; I desperately missed the energy of the city and people watching.

Hebrew School rescued me. Highland Park at the time had a very basic Jewish education program, "synagogue light." So my parents decided I would go by train into Chicago after school to continue my studies at the yeshiva on the North Side at Farwell and Sheridan. I did this on four weekdays and on Sundays. I resented having to study Hebrew while my friends were out playing ball and horsing around. I was twelve and I just hated it.

But I *loved* the experience of going back into the city. My first day on the train, there were eight seventeen-year-old Catholic girls from Wilmette who attended Woodlands Academy of the Sacred Heart in Lake Forest. After about a week, every time I got on the train, they'd be in the same car waiting for me, and we'd ride together for about a half hour. They adopted me as their mascot. I had a more serious approach to life than most twelve-year-old boys, and I think that helped me connect with them. But I was after all still a twelve-year-old boy, and as you can imagine, their company made getting to the yeshiva a lot more fun.

After Hebrew school let out, I was free. I had time to walk around the city. The limitless stimuli of the streets provided tremendous exposure for me. That's when I really fell in love with Chicago. The city was *enticing.* It was crowded and fast and fascinating, with colorful shops and people and all kinds of sights, smells, and sounds that Highland Park didn't have. It challenged my perspective and shaped it in ways that further encouraged me to think beyond the norm.

It also led to my first entrepreneurial adventure. On one of my walks I discovered a newsstand underneath the "L" tracks. It was 1953, and a provocative new magazine called *Playboy* had just made its debut featuring Marilyn Monroe on the cover. It sold for 50 cents. I bought a copy and thought it was terrific. So I brought it home to Highland Park, where it wasn't for sale, and showed it to my friends. One of them offered to buy it. "Three bucks," I said. After that, I started a little magazine import business and, in the process, learned a lasting business lesson: Where there is scarcity, price is no object. This basic tenet of supply and demand would later become a governing principle of my investment philosophy.

I entered my teen years with what I look back on as an unusual maturity and perspective, and it often made relating to and sharing ideas with my friends a challenge. Someone once told me, "Sam, you were born old," and I think that is true. My friends' world experiences seemed narrower than mine. Their parents weren't pushing them the way mine were. They weren't drilling into them that having fun was frivolous. With the guys, this divergence didn't matter much because we connected through sports, and I was passionate about baseball and football—although I was bored by the lengthy discussions about the minute details of each game. With girls, my point of reference was my mother and sisters, highly intelligent women who talked about world affairs, politics and business. (Maybe that's why I have little patience for small talk; I didn't then and I don't today.) I tended to like girls who were smart and interesting, like the women in my house.

This led to an epiphany when I was fourteen and a freshman in high school. I was having lunch with about a dozen guys, and they were going back and forth, talking about copping a feel and who did what to whom, and it hit me that I was put off. I liked girls. You bet. But I had no interest in being part of this type of conversation. In the abstract? Fine. But when it came to my specific relationships? No way; I was very guarded. The teen years are usually all about fitting in, but in that moment I discovered that fitting in just wasn't important to me. I was more comfortable standing apart than I was in searching for a common denominator with others. I could embrace my tendency to go against conventional wisdom. And it would later end up defining my career.

There was another pivotal discovery I made around this time as well. I learned I was a leader. Instead of being part of a crowd, subject to directions I didn't care for, I could set the course. And I could get others to follow me.

I was twelve when I started going to Camp Ramah, a Hebrew-speaking Jewish summer camp in northern Wisconsin. The camp was only six years old then, but it's still there today. In fact, a number of my grandchildren have gone there as well. When I went, there were about 125 kids, and it was a transformative experience for me. The camp was structured, or I should say unstructured, just enough to bring out the kids' natural skill sets.

Ramah was unique in that it treated campers as adults from day one. It just was assumed we were all responsible citizens. For an independent kid who hated restraints, it was heaven. The youngest to the oldest kids all interfaced. So there were no established groups. No one had a predetermined position. It was my first real experience with a meritocracy. All of a sudden I had a blank canvas. In ordinary life I couldn't always get things done the way I wanted. I ran into school politics, parental hurdles and other obstacles. But camp was different. For eight weeks each year, I was an unchecked leader. It did an enormous amount to build my confidence, and it gave me a glimpse of bigger possibilities for my future. I was as good at leading the other kids astray as anything else, but I led them nonetheless.

By the time I was seventeen and a junior counselor, I was pretty full of myself. I became friends with another junior counselor, and we both had the same day off. Twenty-four hours of complete freedom when no one asked where we were. So we started hitchhiking all over the state of Wisconsin. One time we lost track of time and ended up in Florence, Wisconsin, around midnight when there were no more cars on the road. We didn't know what to do, so we walked over to a used car lot, opened up a car, and went to sleep. Exploring is great, but you gotta be able to get back home.

People always want to know whether I am "self-made." Usually when they ask the question, they mean were my parents rich? The answer is no, my parents weren't rich. When they got to the United States they had about the equivalent of $10,000 today. As I was growing up, my father reestablished himself as a successful entrepreneur. And by the time he died, my parents were wealthy, partly because of my father's business and partly because of my own. But the question is still interesting, because they actually left me with so much more than money. It was an inheritance of intelligence, curiosity, drive, resilience, and self-determination. They instilled in me a commitment to learning and an understanding of how to apply it in real life, to challenge convention—to leave when others stay, to be aware of risk and prepare for it. I certainly feel "self-made" in one sense, but in another I recognize the incredible contribution of my parents in shaping my values and success.

My parents wanted me to have a *profession*. To them it was added financial security—something to fall back on if the worst happened. At one point, I actually considered being a rabbi. My father was horrified. He thought being a rabbi was the worst job in the world. He couldn't understand how that would be a job for a good Jewish boy. There were many conversations with my father on this topic. I was exploring my options.

I didn't know where I was headed, but, as always, I was very eager to get there.

CHAPTER TWO

Start by Being Audacious

I didn't plan to start my career while I was in college. It was just something to do. An idea presented itself and I went for it.

I entered the University of Michigan in 1959 as a political science major. I pledged Alpha Epsilon Pi and a year later moved into the fraternity house, which was kind of like a precursor to a scene out of *Animal House*. It was a free-for-all. The wisdom of crowds sometimes means finding the lowest common denominator. Almost overnight my grades slipped, and keeping kosher became virtually impossible. Worse, there was absolutely zero privacy. Personal space simply did not exist. For a loner like me, this was a problem, so I moved out six weeks later to an off-campus apartment. There, it was also easier to have friends from different groups, not just from AE Pi.

I was a restless student, not a great academic. In contrast, both of my sisters excelled; they were both Phi Beta Kappas and earned straight As. I think my parents were really concerned that their only son wasn't measuring up. At one point my father even offered me $5 for every A I could get. What he really didn't understand was that I had no appetite for academics. But I was highly motivated to not let my parents down and was very aware of the benchmark set by my overachieving sisters. Nevertheless, I did get a D one year in accounting. It wasn't that I didn't understand the principles. I did. It was the adherence to stupid rules that drove me crazy. I remember one exam where I wrote "revenues" in a column related to "sales," and the professor marked it as incorrect. "Why is it wrong?" I asked. "Revenues and sales are the same thing." But he had no interest in the meaning of the words; it was about conforming. "If you don't write 'sales' it's wrong." Well, to me, learning by rote was *wrong*.

In my free time I played football and baseball, dated a lot, and got involved with campus events, frivolous activities, per my father. But he and I had very different definitions of freedom.

Mine included my red Cushman Motor Scooter. Parking on campus was a problem; only seniors and grad students were granted parking permits, so most undergrads walked or rode bicycles. I had my scooter. It fed my nomadic tendencies and was the genesis of a lifelong love affair with motorcycles. Later on, of course, my bikes got faster and more expensive. About twenty years after college, I started taking motorcycle trips with a group of friends, most of whom were also business colleagues, and we dubbed ourselves the Zell's Angels. We still do two trips a year, one with just the boys and one with the wives. We ride all over the world, looking for twisty, turny roads and gorgeous landscapes. To me motorcycles physically represent freedom. I love living in my helmet for a week. There's no better way to clear my head; I think of nothing but the road and where I'm going.

Anyway, after sophomore year ended, I was nineteen and I wanted to do something other than Hebrew camp for the summer. Knowing my parents, the only way they'd agree was if it was somehow or other educational. If the word "education" was involved, I could jump off the Empire State Building and they'd be okay with it. So I enrolled at UCLA for the summer, and a friend went with me. It was a six-week course, and I told my parents it was eight. I was going to use the extra two weeks to hitchhike across the country. I don't know if it was rebellion or deference, but I didn't want them to worry so I never told them about the trip. I do know that it was a two-week adventure that was too good to pass up.

My buddy and I left Los Angeles and in seventeen days we traveled some eight thousand miles; we got over two hundred rides.

A surprising number of people were willing to pick up two guys in Bermuda shorts and Michigan sweatshirts. And they were so kind. They took us to their homes, bought us dinners and hotel rooms, and even taught us to water ski. The trip had an enormous impact on my life. It was such an outlier experience and truly extraordinary connection to America. It also gave me one particular epiphany that still influences how I meet with people.

When we reached New York, my friend and I separated and I started to make my way back to Chicago. The first ride I got was from a guy headed west through the mountains on the Pennsylvania Turnpike. It was ninety-five degrees. We were driving along near a wooded area, and as we went through a tunnel, the radiator overheated. Water and steam were spilling all over the place. I was thinking, "Shit, I've just lost my ride." The driver pulled over without saying a word. This was one of those guys who didn't talk much. Some people who would pick you up were like that. You'd sit with them for hours and not a word. The guy got out of the car, walked to the rear, opened the trunk, took out a gas can, and then proceeded to walk straight into the forest. Huh? So I followed him. We walked maybe 150 yards, right off the road, straight into the trees. All of a sudden, there was this beautiful brook. The guy bent down, filled his gas can, walked back to the car, put the water in the radiator, and everything was fine. We got in the car and just started driving again. I was speechless. I finally turned to him and asked, "How did you know?" And I'll never forget it, he just looked at me and said, "Well, I didn't know there was a brook there, but we were in the mountains, so there had to be a water source close by. I figured I'd just walk until I found it."

Well, as a Jewish boy who grew up in Highland Park, there was no way in the world I would have *conceivably* thought of that solution. If my car overheated, I'd have waved someone down and had them call a tow truck. That guy had a sense of logic and orientation that was completely foreign to me. He never had a doubt. Priceless.

That experience never left me. It was a lesson in the value of how much you learn by seeing people in their own environments. Today I could probably get just about anybody to come to my office for a meeting, but that wouldn't tell me much. Instead, I spend over a thousand hours a year on my plane traveling around the world to meet with people. I want to see what they are like on their home court, how they treat their people and the examples they set.

One day, in the middle of my junior year, I was at a friend's apartment and he mentioned that his landlord had just bought the house next door. They were going to knock down both houses to build a fifteen-unit student housing apartment building.

"Let's pitch them to manage it," I said. "Who better than us? We're students; we know what students want. We'll run the building, maintain it, and each get a free apartment."

We didn't know how to manage or rent apartments. We had no clue what it entailed. It just never occurred to me that I couldn't do it. If you're not aware that you're not supposed to be able do something, the barriers to doing it are dramatically lessened. It didn't matter that students hadn't done it before, or that the role was always performed by professional management companies. That desire to take a risk, to test my limits, to ask "Why not?" was part of my DNA, and I don't think I've changed that much since.

So we created a simple brochure and went to pitch the owners. Amazingly, they bought our act. We ended up completely redesigning the interior of their units. The owners had ordered this outdated, horrendous furniture, the kind of stuff you'd find in your grandmother's home. Not at all appealing to college-age kids. We didn't know what we were doing, but we knew that the last thing students wanted was an environment like home. We wanted the exact opposite! At the time, the definition of cool was Scandinavian, so we sent everything they had ordered back and bought furniture with clean, modern lines. We operated strictly on logic and gut, and it worked. That management contract was my first real estate project.

The same landlord built a second student apartment building and gave it to us to manage as well, and then he gave us a third. We brought in my buddy Bob Lurie, who became our first employee, to help us. Bob was famous for carrying IBM punch cards in his breast pocket and always using them to make lists. He was a calm, pragmatic, behind-the-scenes planner who kept a mental record of every detail. Bob was a strong complement to my lack of interest in operational detail, as well as my energy and intensity. We were both self-assured, industrious, independent thinkers who had an aversion to conformity and didn't care much what others thought. We also shared a sense of maturity, of responsibility, and a self-deprecating sense of humor. It was clear right away that we were a great team.

Aside from managing apartments, I continued to come up with different ideas for businesses. One of my side projects was selling gifts for my frat brothers' prom dates. The most popular was a ten-foot-long stuffed smiling snake with a fraternity ribbon tied around its neck. So around dance time my apartment would be filled with boxes of snakes and ribbons, and I'd be sitting there tying them all on. I didn't think anything of it, but I was driven to be productive. From my parents I had learned that economic success equals freedom, even if mine was on a much smaller scale.

Despite all those businesses, I only had one "job" while I was in college. During the summers of my junior and senior years, I was a traveling salesman for Helene Curtis, and I sold to drugstores and supermarkets. I didn't know anything about cosmetics when I started out, but I knew something about selling and I was a fast learner. Because I was a summer employee, I got all of the worst assignments. If you've never sold anything through cold calls or without appointments, it may be hard to imagine, but I can promise you that it's humbling. Most responses are no. Some emphatic, some *really* emphatic. You just build up a tolerance for rejection. You learn to keep asking and to find ways to get a conversation going. If you can just start and keep a dialogue, you have a chance.

I drove a couple thousand miles, without air-conditioning, and it was *hot*. Every day, when 4:30 p.m. came, I'd have to decide—was I going to make one more call? And I always did. I was determined to get the best sales numbers those crappy accounts had ever generated. I also wanted to leave an impression, and to pay back the guys who gave me the opportunity of a job in the first place.

While I was unaware of it at the time, my real compensation for that job wasn't monetary. It was learning about and getting comfortable with rejection. And as I would later realize, indifference to rejection is a fundamental part of being an entrepreneur.

I got married ten days after graduating. My wife, Janet, and I first met while she was dating one of my fraternity brothers. The following year we starting dating. We were married about two years later and moved into an apartment building that I managed.

By then I was solid in my understanding of myself as a business owner. But it was still a sideline for me. Remember, my parents had instilled the belief that I needed a profession, and that was my course. So I went to the University of Michigan Law School. Well, I hated it. I had been in school for what felt like a long time already, and law school was boring beyond belief. I just wasn't built for the arcane attention to detail and the endless rules and subrules and sub-subrules.

Of course later, especially when my deals started to get more complex, I realized my legal education was invaluable; it taught me how to assess, how to think, and where to draw the line. Every day, even today, I use it. I've spent my whole career challenging conventional wisdom and creating my own playbook. You can't do that unless you understand the rules of the game and play well within the lines. It would be like a guy playing football and not knowing where the line of scrimmage is set. As long as you know where everyone else is, you can play the game. As a result, I became a huge advocate of law school, with the caveat that it is numbingly boring. My real estate deals during that time were what kept me sane.

I bought my first building in Ann Arbor in 1965, during my second year of law school. It was a three-unit apartment building, 912 Sybil Street. I bought it for $19,500 with $1,500 down, which I had saved from our apartment management business. I repainted the interior, replaced all the furniture, and doubled the rents. A couple of months later, I bought another building nearly next door, and then I bought the house in between. I had some money saved from my various ventures, and I was able to bootstrap my way into these early deals with a combination of savings and bank loans.

The third acquisition was a big single-family house. I found an architect, a small local general contractor, and we created a design for four separate units. Then I went to the bank and got loans to do the renovation. I was twenty-three, with a BA in political science. I didn't know anything about financing. But it never crossed my mind that I might be too young to start an investment business or that I couldn't do it. I didn't know any better, but was able to sell the banks on my ability to get it done. Our management company took over the property, did the renovation, and rented the units. The asset did very well.

Then we landed a huge management contract for a project in Ypsilanti at Eastern Michigan University. The deal changed the landscape for us—both in opportunity and risk. Our new scale made us a relevant factor in the local real estate market. And that reputation led to a call later that year from a friend of mine who had graduated and was clerking for a judge. He asked me for advice about a property. His father had bought him a house off campus on Geddes Street and he had just gotten an offer from a local developer to buy it for $3 a square foot for the land. What should he do?

I said, "I really don't know, but I'll check it out." So, I called some local real estate guys to get an idea of the property's value. One of the guys was Don Chisholm. I learned the site could support $3.50 a square foot, and Chisholm and I decided to bid. I called my friend back and said, "Chisholm and I will give you $3.50." And we did the deal. But the site wasn't big enough to build a building. At the time, you couldn't develop a new building in Ann Arbor unless it was on a double lot, so I told Chisholm, "Let's see if we can buy the house next door." And we did. Then I said, "Let's keep going," and we proceeded to buy another house on the block, and then another.

I was the pitchman. I went to each of the houses, sat on a lot of couches, and flipped through dozens of family photo albums as I explained to the homeowners that we were going to build student housing and they could either stay and put up with loud music at night and beer cans on the lawn, or they could move to the other side of Ann Arbor. It worked. I kept buying houses and eventually acquired one full block of land. They were all cash deals, $1,000 each to tie up the properties with deferred closings requiring around $20,000.

Along the way, I learned something about people I'll never forget. I was trying to buy the next house in the succession of acquisitions, and the owners said, "You just paid eighteen thousand dollars for the house next door, and you're only offering us eighteen thousand, but our house is a lot nicer."

"But I'm just buying the land; it's an assemblage for a development," I explained. "I will be tearing the house down, so it doesn't matter that it is nicer."

"But our house is worth a lot more. You've got to pay us more," they argued.

"If I pay you more, then the people next door will come back and want more money too," I replied.

And then they said, "Pay us more, and we won't tell them."

I was stunned. I wasn't naïve, but that was a lesson in human nature that was completely foreign to me and the way I was raised. These people had been friends and neighbors for twenty-five years, and for $1,000, they were willing to throw their neighbors under the bus. I ended up paying them the original price I offered. They could fool their neighbors, but I wasn't going to. The idea that I was supposed to lie to the people next door—I would never do that. I've never forgotten that experience.

In 1965, in the middle of our efforts to acquire the buildings on Geddes, Chisholm was called to the National Guard for the summer. By the time he came back, I had put down payments on eight houses at $1,000 each. But we didn't have the money to close. We needed $160,000, $60,000 of which was equity. Needing capital, I invited my father to come to Ann Arbor. Over the years, he had become a successful investor in real estate, and I had kept him apprised of what I was doing.

My father drove to Ann Arbor and I showed him the properties. Then I took him to meet Chisholm, who told my father that he wanted him to buy a one-third stake. My father refused. He wanted a fifty-fifty deal and that was his condition. Chisholm said he'd think it over and we left the meeting. As we were driving back to my father's hotel, we saw a car following us. When we pulled in, the car came up behind us and Chisholm jumped out. He walked up to my father with his hand out for a shake. "Mr. Zell," he said, "fifty percent it is." Being able to invite my father to participate in this investment, and his willingness to do so, were big confidence builders. Like any kid, I wanted my father's approval, and knowing that he viewed me as a legitimate businessman was a milestone for me. He was a gruff guy—stoic in an old-world way. He would never say he thought I had done well, so I learned to appreciate the small signs that I had his blessing.

The last property I wanted on that block was a double lot. Every developer in town had been trying to buy it because it was buildable on its own, but no one could figure out how. I refused to accept that it couldn't be done. It was simply a problem to be solved—an invitation to look at things a different way. For me that has always been where the fun starts.

The property was occupied by Mrs. D, a fifty-five-year-old woman, and her sixty-year-old husband, a stockman at Hoover Ball and Bearing Company. But the property was owned by Mrs. D's wealthy uncle in Chicago. He let his niece live there because she had cared for his ailing mother, who was now deceased and buried in the cemetery across the street.

I visited Mrs. D and gave her the pitch. I explained that it was in her best interest to sell because I was going to build a large student housing complex on the block. I painted the picture for her—loud parties, etc. On the other hand, with the value of her property, she could buy something much better on the other side of town. She explained that her uncle owned the house and I'd have to talk to him. He was the president of a large public energy company, and he lived in the Chicago area—in Winnetka's very upscale neighborhood, Indian Hills. This was the roadblock all the other developers who had tried to buy the property had encountered.

So, I called the uncle and arranged to meet him at his home in Winnetka. I told him, "Look, I own all of the surrounding property. I'm going to build an apartment building and it will be full of students. Your niece is fifty-five, her husband is sixty. The house is about a hundred years old and falling apart. Let's find her another, bigger, better house on the other side of town for the same value and do a tax-free swap."

He nodded. "If you can arrange it so I don't have to put any money up, and I don't have to pay taxes, I'll do it. The only criterion is that you have to make her happy."

I figured the deal was as good as done, and I returned to Ann Arbor and identified five houses that were all in the same price range for what I was going to pay for the land, about $32,000 to $34,000. These five houses were beautiful—every one of them was three times better than what Mrs. D lived in. One day I drove her around to see them. She walked through each one but never said a word. I couldn't get any response at all. At the end of the day, I drove her back home. As we neared the corner by her house, we saw a man swaying and holding onto a lamppost. I pointed him out, and Mrs. D said, "Oh, that's my brother. He lives with us and visits the bars every night. That's why I don't like any of the houses we went to see—because he can't drive; he has to be within at least eight blocks of the downtown bars because he goes there every night, gets drunk, and then walks home."

That's what we call the major unknown factor.

"No problem," I said to Mrs. D, for the first of many times.

I went back to the multiple listings I had reviewed previously, and I found a sixth house to show her that was eight blocks from town. I thought it was perfect. It was on a double lot, identical in size to what she had. It had new heating and electrical, and it was only $19,000. I took her to see it, and she liked it, so we started the process. But the next day Mrs. D called me. "Mr. Zell, my husband and I have been talking, and we have decided we don't want my brother to live in the house with us anymore."

"No problem," I said. "There's an apartment on the second floor. We'll fix it up and he can live alone."

"That won't work," she said. "He can't manage the stairs. There's no way he can climb them after he's been out drinking all night."

"No problem," I said.

So, I went and consulted with the contractor and we discovered that the basement in the house had fourteen-foot-high ceilings. We designed a perfect one-bedroom apartment for Mrs. D's brother. He'd be able to walk down five steps and be home. As a bonus, there would still be an apartment above the garage that she could rent for extra income.

"Okay," she said.

We finished the design and scheduled a contractor to start working on a Monday at 7:00 a.m. At 11:00 on Sunday night, Mrs. D called. "Mr. Zell, my husband and I have been talking, and we just can't have my brother living in a basement. It's not right and we'll feel guilty."

"No problem," I said. "I'll be over tomorrow and we'll figure it out."

Since the purchase price was only $19,000, and the house was on a double lot, we had more options available. I proposed that we build a one-bedroom apartment extension onto the house, side by side. We could design it so that if her brother walked in the front door of his unit and kept walking, he'd end up in the shower. She loved it. And I had completed my acquisition of the last parcel I needed to own the whole block.

I remember this event so clearly because it was at this point in my career that I fully realized the value of tenacity. I just had to assume there was a way through any obstacle, and then I'd find it. This is perhaps my most fundamental principle of entrepreneurialism, and to success in general.

But my experience with Mrs. D was also about the value of

really *listening*, which is at the heart of any negotiation. Understanding what's truly important to the other person out of the dozen or so things they might tell you. Mrs. D's brother had to be taken care of. That was her bottom line. Homing in on that got the deal done.

Later that week, we hosted a 1960s-style "free art" party. We removed the old cans of paint from the basements of the houses we'd bought and brought them all to one house. About thirty of us went nuts throwing paint on the walls and creating our own house-size Jackson Pollock. It was radical fun—a playful and completely irreverent ending to a very arduous process.

In total, we ended up owning about a dozen houses, all adjacent. It was the largest block of land held by one owner near campus. We sold the site the following year for well above what we paid for the buildings in aggregate. The buyer built a large apartment building complex on Geddes Avenue, between Linden and Oxford, which is still there today.

This series of acquisitions and the assets' subsequent sale was my first exposure to the benefits of scale. With each additional house we acquired, we expanded the aggregate site's ability to accommodate a larger, more efficient and economically viable development. By assembling the pieces, we had made the whole more valuable. This was a meaningful takeaway, and the exponential value of scale would influence my assessment of investment opportunities—in and outside of real estate—throughout my career.

At the end of my last year of law school, I went back to Chicago for vacation, sat down with my father, and asked him to tell me about his real estate deals. By then he had reestablished himself as a successful businessman who, like others of his generation, had accumulated capital and then invested in real estate through syndicators. He told me he was getting about a 4 percent return on apartments and net leases, which was de rigueur for the time. All of the assets they bought were in major cities like New York, Los Angeles, San Francisco, and Chicago. They never went anywhere else. While their strategy was a safe bet, it was also limiting. The cost of construction was significantly less in smaller cities like Ann Arbor and—even more important—there was no competition. But the syndicators didn't know those second- and third-tier cities even existed. So there was no real capital looking for assets in those smaller markets. Without competition, I could set the price—and the market.

That was my first real investment thesis. If I could replicate what I was doing in Ann Arbor in other markets, I could realize some serious upside. I would build a portfolio of assets in smaller, high-growth markets with a focus on university towns. That all seems logical in hindsight today, but back then nobody was doing it.

I graduated from law school in 1966. I was twenty-four. I had $250,000 in the bank, and I had made about $150,000 that year. (That was an income of about $1.1 million in 2016.) I had established a solid foundation for my family—which was good, because that year my son, Matthew, was born. Two years later, my daughter, JoAnn, followed.

I thought about whether I should stay in Ann Arbor and keep going or if I should try something new. I concluded that if I stayed, I would just be a big fish in a small pond. I needed to find out how good I was, and I couldn't do that in a college town. If I didn't test my limits, how would I ever know what I could do? So, my partner and I sold our business to Bob Lurie, and I headed home to Chicago.

CHAPTER THREE

My Own Rules

I hit Chicago ready to start my "profession" in the law. Of course, my plan was to continue to do real estate deals on the side. I thought I'd have no trouble finding a job with a good law firm. But after my forty-third rejection, I was beginning to wonder. I couldn't figure out what the problem was. I hadn't been a great student, but I'd graduated in the top quarter of my class at the University of Michigan Law School, which had a very good reputation. It didn't make any sense. Finally, I got a meeting with Charles Kaufman, a founder and senior partner of Vedder, Price, Kaufman in Chicago, which had about 150 lawyers. When his secretary ushered me into his office, he was on the phone and he motioned me to sit down. He finished his phone call, got up and closed the door, then sat across from me. He gave me a funny look.

"Tell me about your deals," he said.

"What?" I was taken aback. "I'm here for a job!"

He waved his hand dismissively and said, "Oh, we'd never hire you. You'd last maybe three months and then you'd go back to doing deals."

As I was trying to take this in and prepare myself for another rejection, he explained, "I looked at your resume and I've never seen anything like this. You're not going to be a lawyer, you're going to be a deal guy. We would just be wasting our time if we hired you, because we'd train you and you wouldn't stick around."

So now I knew why I kept getting turned down. My resume was focused on my business experience, not on my legal education. I had thought law firms would be impressed with what I had accomplished, that my deals would give me an edge. What I didn't understand was they were a red flag that I'd never be happy in a law firm. Kaufman was right, of course, but it took me a little longer to catch on.

I ended up working at a small firm, Yates & Holleb, in Chicago. It was the first and only "job" of my career. I lasted four days. I spent them laboring over a contract between a linen supply company and Northern Illinois University. It was horrendous, just excruciating. On the fifth day, I went in to see my boss, the junior partner, Bob Michaelson, and told him—as only a twenty-four-year-old can do—that I didn't think writing legal contracts was really a good use of my time.

After he recovered from my audacity, Bob said, "What are you going to do?"

"I'm going back to doing deals," I replied.

He said, "Well, then, why don't you just keep doing deals? We'll invest and do the legal work, and you can keep an office here."

That sounded like a good idea, so I agreed. The arrangement was that I'd get 50 percent of any legal business I brought in. This was their standard commission, and it was designed to encourage young lawyers toward rainmaking—so they'd bring new business into the firm. It was *not* designed for a large volume of new business—which they quickly realized when their payouts to me grew at what to them was an alarming rate. Within four weeks, I was bringing in so much new legal work from my deals they reduced my commission to 35 percent. Within the year my cut was down to 25 percent.

One evening in December, as I neared my eighteen-month anniversary, a junior partner called me into his office. "I just found out how much you made this year," he said, giving me the once-over. He seemed pissed off about it. "Look," he said, "if I stopped practicing law and just got on the phone with brokers, I could do that too." That's when I realized he had no idea what I did. He thought I just sat on the phone and flipped deals. Here he was practicing law, working eighty hours a week, and making $25,000 a year, while this twenty-five-year-old kid was making more than three times that. The conversation was a revelation. Until then I hadn't recognized that my career was so radically different from the mainstream. I had thought I was just off-center; I hadn't realized I was on a completely different road. But that partner's perspective jarred me into an epiphany—I had to leave the law firm.

I remember coming home after I quit. My wife, Janet, was pregnant. "You quit?!" she asked, alarmed. "What are you going to do?"

"Just do what I do," I replied. My answer wasn't all that comforting to her, and I couldn't really articulate it, but I knew exactly what I meant. My orientation toward being an outlier was going to define my future. I was going to do what I loved doing, and I wasn't going to be encumbered by anyone else's rules. So I left Yates & Holleb and opened my business in a spare office at my brother-in-law Roger's law firm at 10 South LaSalle Street. That was the precursor to the investment firm I still run today.

My investment thesis was still based on targeting small,

high-growth cities where there was no competing capital. I continued buying apartment properties in university towns because that's where the opportunity was. Schools in the country were growing. And the largest fixed costs of real estate—taxes and utilities—were lower in these second-tier cities, so the net margins were significantly higher. I had about twenty investors, including my father, a few of his colleagues, and some attorneys from Yates & Holleb.

In 1966, I closed on my first major asset, which I had started working on while still in Ann Arbor. It was a $1 million, ninety-nine-unit apartment building across the street from the University of Toledo in Ohio. University Park Apartments was right in line with my experience, and I believed the yield on the deal would be 19 percent. I brought the opportunity to my father, and he had a property management guy, Arthur Mohl, review it. Arthur recut all my numbers and concluded that the deal would yield an 8 percent return, which was still terrific at the time. So Arthur recommended the investment to my father and then put up some of his own money. The asset immediately produced a cash flow at double the level Arthur projected and ended up producing a 20 percent return. When I went to do my second big deal, the same investors, along with some of their buddies, stood in line. After that, the line was around the block.

My deals, of course, got much bigger, much more sophisticated—and by nature held more risk. My father liked the old way, so eventually he bowed out. We just had fundamentally different approaches, and I left him to pursue my own.

From Toledo, we went into Tampa, Orlando, and Jacksonville, Florida; Arlington, Texas; and Reno, Nevada. Don Chisholm, my co-investor from Ann Arbor, introduced me to the opportunity in Reno. He called me from an appraisal class he was taking in San

Francisco. "Sam, I had a conversation with this guy from Carson City [Nevada] at lunch yesterday. I was telling him about our deals in Michigan and he told me he's got a 160-unit apartment project for sale in Reno, Nevada. What do you think?"

I didn't know . . . *Reno?* It was all about easy divorces and gambling, right? But I've always been a believer in exploring every opportunity. So I told Chisholm, "Since you're so close, why don't you go over there and check it out?"

Chisholm headed to Reno, took a look, and called me back. "Sam, this is a great city. It's growing like crazy. The building is fully occupied and throwing off a nineteen percent return, cash on cash."

Cash on cash. Income earned on cash invested. Not dependent on appreciation, just cash. And with a high rate of return, so we would be paid for the risk of an unknown market. We did that deal, and we ended up buying three or four other buildings in Reno. Then we did some more deals in Florida with the same sellers.

I like doing deals with the same people. You get to know each other and build a mutual sense of trust. Today, a lot of what I do originates from associations that go back ten, twenty, thirty, even forty years. Anyway, the returns from the Reno deal were every bit as good as I projected, if not better.

One day in 1969, I was sitting in my office at seven in the morning and I got a phone call from Stan Weingast, a broker I knew in New York. He told me he'd just spent the day with Jay Pritzker and that Jay was looking for a successful entrepreneur in real estate, a lawyer, under thirty to come work for him. Stan immediately thought of me.

Everyone knew the Pritzkers. They were one of the most prominent business families in Chicago, and they had started the Hyatt Hotel chain. Jay Pritzker was legendary in the investment world. He had built and now controlled a staggering empire. Jay was one of only a few people who would make a decision overnight to invest huge amounts of money. His liquidity and financial relationships made him the go-to guy of his era.

The idea of meeting Jay Pritzker was intriguing to me, but I already knew I didn't want to work for anyone. When Stan Weingast suggested it, I said, "If I meet the requirements of being a successful real estate entrepreneur and attorney, why would I want to work for Pritzker or anybody else?"

"Look," Stan said, "Jay is an extraordinary human being, and you need to meet him."

So, the next morning I went over to see Jay. I got there about nine in the morning, and I didn't leave until four thirty that afternoon.

After his father, A. N. Pritzker, grilled me for about an hour, I sat in Jay's office as he took calls and we discussed various deals. It was fascinating to listen to him. At lunch, he gave me the full sales pitch: "Look at what we have here, the resources we have, you could come here and do deals, and you'd end up with five percent." Five percent! I laughed and said, "Oh, so that's a Pritzker deal!" He didn't laugh.

But I stayed and we kept talking. Truth is, Jay and I instantly clicked. As I was sitting there getting to know Jay, I was having fun, even though I still knew I wouldn't take the job.

Finally, at the end of the day, I said, "Jay, I'm not going to work for you or anybody else. So why don't we just do a deal together?"

And he said, "Fine."

"I've made a loan on a property in Lake Tahoe," I said. "I think there's an extraordinary opportunity to buy and develop the site."

Jay didn't even hesitate. "Okay," he said. "Let's do it."

I left and took the elevator. When the doors opened on the ground floor, A. N. Pritzker was standing there. He looked surprised to see me. "Were you with my son all this time?"

I said, "Yeah."

He said, "By now you could have built a building!"

That meeting with Jay was the beginning of the most influential relationship of my career, apart from the ones with my father and Bob Lurie. Jay was the smartest financial guy I ever met. He taught me how to look at deals and how to focus on what would either make them or break them. He introduced me to new ways of looking at opportunities and transactions. He became my mentor and my friend. We thought so similarly we could have been related. In fact, Jay, who was nineteen years older, used to joke that when he was my age, he used to play the field and that I must have been the result of one of his indiscretions.

Our project in Lake Tahoe was the second of only two projects that I had ever developed from scratch. When I had left my four-day stint as an attorney, I decided that in addition to buying existing properties, I would become a developer. In fact, my thought was that I was going to create the General Motors of the housing industry.

The Tahoe project was located on beautiful land at the base of the mountains. Since the building season there was short, I had the idea of building prefabricated units elsewhere, which then would be trucked in and erected during the few best building months in Tahoe. After the project was largely assembled, I showed up to walk the site. The ground floor looked great, but when I went up to the second floor, it was really dark. And I realized the contractor had mistakenly built the eaves too long. They extended past the windows. So instead of beautiful mountain views, the windows looked out onto the inside of the roof! We ended up solving the problem by cutting "windows" into the roof to save the views. But it was a debacle, and it came on the heels of my first apartment complex development project in Lexington, Kentucky. I had been blindsided by a terrible mistake in the building plans on that project as well. When the project was about 80 percent completed, I had done a walk-through of the units and I was baffled by what I saw. On one side of the building the units were extraordinarily small, and on the other side they were extraordinarily large. When I consulted the building plans, I discovered a waste pipe in the center of the building. Only it wasn't in the center; it was off by about 20 percent, and the builder had built to those incorrect specifications. We were too far along to correct it, so I ended up renting the small units for less and the larger units for more. The project did reasonably well, but it wasn't at all what we expected.

By the time I got through both of those projects, I realized development was more complex and risky than I had thought. In addition to problems with the blueprints, city regulators can change the game midstream with new fees and costs; the economy can shift, causing tenant demand to evaporate during the time it takes to get the building up; banks can come down on you; and on and on.

As a result, I was cured of any inclination to become a developer. I think that to stay in that business, most developers must get 50 percent of their returns from real cash flow and the other 50 percent from the intangible benefit of seeing their phallic symbols rise out of the ground. Otherwise I can't see the reward.

My takeaway was a whole new respect for simplicity. Development required multiple steps, and every step meant one more chance for something to go wrong.

When Jay and I liquidated the Tahoe investment years later, I noticed that we had forgotten something critical, so I called him. "Listen," I said, "the deal is closed, but I just realized we never drew up a formal partnership agreement between the two of us. If the IRS comes and reviews this thing, we're going to look like idiots if we don't have documents."

"Yeah, yeah," he said, not really interested. That was indicative of Jay. Trust was one of his abiding principles. He'd always bet a lot more on the person than on the deal. Once Jay decided that I was honest and smart, he was on board. He never called me to check on things. He never questioned where we were in our investment. The title to the property was in my name. At the same time, I had no doubt that if it all went south at any time, Jay would have my back.

Jay taught me to use simplicity as a strategy. He had an uncanny ability to grasp an extremely complex situation and immediately locate the weakness. He always said that if there were twelve steps in a deal, the whole thing depended on just one of them. The others would either work themselves out or were less important. He had a laser focus on risk. I like to say my father taught me how to *be*, law school taught me how to *think*, Jay taught me how to *understand risk*.

After the Tahoe deal, we did a series of others. One of them, in 1970, was Broadway Plaza in Los Angeles. Broadway Plaza was a mixed-use complex with 700,000 square feet of office space, 400,000 square feet of retail, and a 500 room Hyatt Hotel. It was a joint venture being developed by Carter Hawley Hale

(CHH) and Ogden Corporation. (As an aside, I ended up owning both of those companies years later.) I started negotiating the deal, which was complex beyond belief. I was creating structures and terms that had never been done before. I went to Jay and took him step-by-step through this incredibly complicated transaction. And damn it if he didn't just look at me and say, "But, Sam, isn't the real key to this whole thing just to rent the office space?" And sure enough, that's what the whole transaction was predicated on.

Jay's level of intellectual rigor really appealed to me. And I immediately latched on to the understanding that I could cut right to the heart of something complex if I broke the problem into pieces. It was a matter of organizing my thinking. A discipline. It brought me back to seventh-grade social studies where I learned how to create an outline. It was the same core concept, just applied at a more sophisticated level. I still apply it today.

Like a lot of deals, Broadway Plaza had to close by the end of the year for tax considerations. And until late in the game the sellers were flirting with other suitors. So we came in with a very tight window. On Tuesday, December 29, I sat down in a conference room with the lawyers and didn't leave for more than forty-eight hours. It was intense and exhausting. At one point I just lost it. I slid under the table and went to sleep while the two lawyers continued to go back and forth above me. I slept for an hour and a half, climbed back up during the conversation, and kept going.

At 2:30 on Thursday afternoon, it was obvious that we were done. While the agreements were being finalized, I went back to the hotel to take a shower and get a haircut before the 5:00 p.m. closing.

I wasn't sure exactly how much cash I would need for the

signing. I knew it was going to be between $8 million and $10 million, but I didn't know the exact amount. So I asked Jay to send me multiple certified checks, and I'd deal with them accordingly.

I was sitting in the barber's chair when a messenger came in and handed me an envelope. I couldn't resist—I opened the envelope and started counting to make sure I had the $10 million. The barber was looking over my shoulder and I swear he clipped my ear! The funny thing is, I looked like shit. I'd been up for two days and I was wearing jeans. The barber had probably been wondering if I was even good for the haircut.

But back to Jay. He was highly competitive. And—this shouldn't be surprising—so am I. But Jay always beat me. We'd play racquetball, he won. Tennis, he won. Even gin rummy, he won. I've often said I was the world's greatest above-average athlete. Any sport, I could play above average. But he kicked my ass in everything. There was only one sport I knew I had over him, and that was skiing. It is the only sport that maybe I seriously excel in. I tend to ski straight down, no turns. I just point my tips down and go, no matter the course. So I was waiting, rather impatiently, for the chance to get Jay on the slopes.

In January 1971, after we closed the Broadway Plaza deal, we decided to go to Snowbird in Utah. I was really excited. I didn't know how good Jay was, but I knew how good *I* was, and I figured the chances of him being better than me were pretty slim.

Our first full day there we were up and on the first tram. At the top I grinned at him and shouted, "Ready? Go!" and down we went. Boom. I was flying down the mountain and about halfway, I turned around and didn't see Jay. I was instantly suspicious that he'd gone the other way around and was going to make a fool out of me, which would have been a typical Jay move. So I sped up and double-timed it the rest of the way. At the bottom there was no Jay. Finally, after about ten minutes he showed up. I immediately started giving him a hard time. I was elated.

"I don't feel terrific," he said. "I want to get a hot chocolate."

I responded the only way a good friend could. "A hot chocolate, my ass! You just don't want to get beaten again." And I went on and on, until I noticed Jay wasn't himself. He had no give-and-take in him. Something was off. So I finally stopped and said, "Okay Jay, let's go get some hot chocolate."

As we were sitting in the café he said he had a stomachache and needed to go get some Pepto-Bismol, but then he didn't come back. After twenty minutes, I went down to the infirmary to check, and there was Jay—with his shirt off and an oxygen mask over his face. He was having a heart attack! I was completely stunned. There I was, twenty-nine years old, on a mountain with Jay Pritzker, and he was having a heart attack. All of a sudden this important guy was my responsibility. What was I supposed to do?

I began making a series of calls to Jay's doctor and people in the Pritzker organization. I watched helplessly as the local doctor examined him, not knowing the quality of care Jay was getting. I told his doctor in Chicago that he needed to get out to Snowbird immediately. He responded, "How am I supposed to get there tonight?" And I told him, "I don't care if you have to charter a plane, just do it." He said, "Okay, I'll call you back." Fifteen minutes later, he called me back and said the Pritzker School of Medicine at the University of Chicago Hospital was going to equip a plane with oxygen and other supplies and he'd be there that night. The plan was to take Jay home where he would be assured of getting the best possible treatment.

I was so relieved. I went back in to Jay and said, "Jay, I just talked to Eddie and he's chartering a plane. He'll be here at nine o'clock." Jay slowly lifted the oxygen mask off his face. He was very pale and very serious. He looked up at me and said, "Couldn't he go commercial?"

Ultimately, Jay ended up staying in Utah and getting excellent treatment there, and he recovered. Two months later, he was back in business, and we went on to do more deals together.

Jay had a profound impact on me personally and professionally. He gave me the incomparable gifts of his support, wisdom, and trust. When he died of heart trouble in 1999 at age seventy-six, it was a great personal loss for me and for everyone who knew him well.

Around the same time I was spending a lot of time with Jay, I read the book *Zeckendorf: The Autobiography of the Man who Played a Real-Life Game of Monopoly and Won the Largest Real Estate Empire in History.* It reinforced the approach of viewing the whole through its individual pieces, but for a different purpose. William Zeckendorf was perhaps one of the greatest real estate developers of the modern era; he is responsible for significant buildings on the Manhattan skyline and a large swath of Chicago's Magnificent Mile. Among other iconic properties, he developed the United Nations building in New York, Century City in Los Angeles, and the Place Ville-Marie in Montreal.

Zeckendorf's autobiography was packed with colorful stories, but what fascinated me most was his strategy. Zeckendorf viewed assets as a sum of parts, so he could increase the value of the whole. Various parts were more valuable to different buyers, so Zeckendorf could maximize the value of his holding overall, in effect making $1 + 1 = 3$. For example, One Park Avenue in Manhattan, which the marketplace had valued at $10 million, was ultimately worth $15 million in Zeckendorf's hands. He calculated everything separately—the building's title, the land, the leases, the individual mortgages. I thought this was brilliant. I adopted the approach both inside and, later, outside of the real estate industry.

By this time, Bob Lurie was my partner. He was, in fact, the closest friend and the only business partner I would ever have. Before I left Ann Arbor in 1966, I had said to Bob, with the hubris of a twenty-four-year-old, "If you get tired of screwing around here and want to come play with the big boys, call me." And in 1969, he did.

"Remember the last thing you said to me?" he asked. By then, Bob had completed a master's degree in mechanical engineering, and the business we had sold him had barely survived a student rent strike. He was ready to leave Michigan behind.

"Yes," I replied.

"I'm ready."

"Come on," I said without hesitation.

So Bob liquidated the apartment management business in Ann Arbor and came to Chicago. Neither of us could have imagined how rich and rewarding our partnership would become.

From the outset, I told Bob that I didn't want him to be an employee. I wanted him to be my partner. We made an amorphous agreement with the vision of eventually reaching an equal partnership. From then on, we divvied up the returns from each deal, and Bob's ownership of our company increased along with the deals and his contributions. At first it was 85/15. By 1974, it was 66/33. By 1976, it was 60/40. And by 1978, it was 50/50. It was a fair deal, based on mutual appreciation for our respective contributions.

I don't know how you can ever have a *real* partner unless you both share the same risk. Bob and I had equal exposure—not at first, but certainly for most of our careers together. When Bob said,

"Let's do this deal," he knew he was putting as much on the line as I was, and vice versa. We had unquestionable, 100 percent trust in each other. We never had a written partnership agreement, and we lived out of the same checkbook. If he was building a new home for his family, he'd take a draw from our joint company money. If I was building a new home for my family, same thing. We never had to account to each other for anything we spent.

Bob and I both saw business as a puzzle to be solved, and we both had an insatiable intellectual curiosity. We had an uncanny way of approaching a problem using completely different methodologies—Bob from the analytical, everything-has-to-balance-out angle, and me from an instinctive, gut-level angle—and reaching the same conclusion. When Bob approached a problem, he'd digest the information, shake it up, and put it back together in an entirely different way. It was amazing to watch. No one was surprised when the Rubik's Cube came out and Bob solved it in ten minutes.

Bob was incisive, introspective, and quirky, with a self-deprecating sense of humor. He was kind of quiet, but could express in one sentence what others could take a paragraph to say.

He spent the first two years of our partnership working in Reno, managing our assets there. While he was there, the engineers' union tried to unionize one of our buildings. It only had thirteen employees, and Bob, as was his nature, knew each one of them personally. The union vote was scheduled for 3:00 p.m. one afternoon. Bob called me at 1:00 and said it was a fait accompli. Not one of our employees was going to vote for the union. Two hours later, he called me back and said we had unanimously lost the vote. It was a lesson neither of us ever forgot, and we referred to it often. The deal's not done until it's done.

In 1971, when Bob returned to Chicago, we moved into larger

office space at 10 South LaSalle. That was when the real growth began for our investment firm, Equity Group Investments (EGI). And EGI would later serve as the base of the broader "Equity" brand we would eventually develop. Today that brand applies to six companies, each worth or managing billions of dollars of assets. We only had about ten employees throughout the early 1970s. At the core were Bob and me; our accountant, Art Greenberg; and our internal auditor, Gerry Spector.

From the beginning, Bob and I believed in creating a meritocracy. EGI was entrepreneurial, based on transparency, initiative, creativity, trust, and the alignment of interests. We paid people enough salary to live comfortably, but all of their ups came from participation in the investments. In other words, the real money was in the deal residuals, the percentage of profits each deal earned, not from salary. There was no cherry-picking of projects, and rewards were found in each year's accomplishments, not in deal-by-deal allocations. Virtually everyone on the team had a piece of everyone else's deal, so while we always had a healthy level of lighthearted internal rivalry, everyone also went out of their way to make sure the other person's deal succeeded. That basic principle has never changed over the decades.

Bob and I originated the unique culture at EGI that became our company trademark. We abandoned all pretense and established a casual-dress office policy—which, believe me, was unheard of in the rigid world of finance in the 1970s. We *invented* business casual. Our thinking was that if you dress funny and you're great at what you do, you're eccentric. But if you dress funny and you're just okay at what you do, you're a schmuck. We were determined to show everyone that we could excel without conforming.

Bob was as iconoclastic as I was. He had long, crazy, wavy, kind-of-frizzy red hair with a receding hairline, long sideburns, and a bushy handlebar mustache and beard. It looked like he had put his finger in a light socket. He wore the same Levi's jeans, the same belt (with a large, silver marijuana-leaf belt buckle), the same plaid shirt, and the same Chippewa boots nearly every day. The only change would be flannel shirts in winter and cotton in summer. He actually bought each of these items in bulk—five to ten at a time—because he was worried one of them might be discontinued. And he would record the date the items were bought on each label in black laundry pen. I remember Bob telling me that when his son, Jessie, was about five, his class was learning words and his teacher held up a picture of a man in a suit, and Jessie didn't know what it was. Of course, what I wore wasn't any more traditional. I liked jeans and Nik Nik shirts—polyester, button-down shirts in wild, bold-color patterns. I had a whole collection of them. For special occasions I'd wear a red leather jumpsuit.

Back then almost no one had heard of us. In 1973, when we bought a large apartment project in Houston, Bob had to travel there to pick up a $1 million wire and go close the deal. I called our Chicago banker and told him, "I'm wiring the money to our account and Lurie is going to pick it up. You'd better tell the banker in Houston what to expect. If he's not prepared and Bob shows up, this deal won't get done. No one at the bank will believe he's there to legitimately pick up $1 million. Tell him Bob will be wearing a plaid shirt, jeans, and boots, and that he has really wild red hair."

Our banker called his counterpart in Houston and wired the $1 million. When Bob walked into the Houston bank, the vice president ran right over to greet him, "Hello, Mr. Lurie!"

Perplexed, Bob looked at him and asked, "How did you know who I was?"

The bank guy answered, "Well, Joe called me and said you

were a colorful character, and you're the first colorful character to walk in here!"

We designed our office space to be as unconventional as our dress—and our deals. The main area walls featured Mylar wallpaper in outrageously bright yellow and other colors. My office was bright red. Howard Walker, one of my attorneys and a longtime friend, once said he felt like he was walking into the inside of a Juicy Fruit wrapper when he visited. Partners and investors referred to our offices as the Wild West. They liked to meet at our place because the setting was fun and offbeat and so inconsistent with the double- and triple-digit returns we were achieving.

Our desks were all in proximity to one another, and no one closed their doors. We always had a background soundtrack of the Rolling Stones, the Beatles, the Mamas and the Papas, and the Fifth Dimension. (Even today if you call our office and get put on hold, you'll hear the Beatles.) People would just yell when they needed someone. "Greenberg, come in here!" Or "Spector!" Or whomever. Our employees would sometimes get unnerved when they were in one of our offices trying to carry on a conversation while simultaneously addressing opposing commentary coming from the neighboring room. But that's the way it was.

Bob was usually the grounding voice of reason in our company. He was Mr. Inside, the operator. I was Mr. Outside, the salesman. I was the optimist, and he was the pessimist, until, of course, I was the pessimist, which compelled him by nature to take the opposite position.

He used to say "Do you know what my job is around here? I say *no*." For emphasis, his office featured a Jasper Johns lithograph on the wall that had a wavy arrow coming down to a point, and underneath it was the word "No." There were times I would rush into Bob's office wildly enthused about a new opportunity, ready to jump, and he would stick a big pin in the balloon. And I'd just move on to the next idea. Our employees used to say Bob was like the mother of our little family and I was like the father.

Bob was known for writing deal structures and other notes on napkins and scratch paper. Someone would ask him a question and he'd pull out all these bits of paper, shuffle through them, and read the answer. He somehow always kept it together and knew where to find whatever he was hunting for.

He was extremely parsimonious and watched every single nickel in our business. Bob was constantly on the lookout for anything that could be reused. He used to walk into somebody's office and, while talking, would casually rummage through the person's trashcan. He'd take out stacks of papers that still had paper clips on them, all while continuing his conversation as though nothing out of the ordinary was occurring. Bob would just pull those paper clips off and hand them back to the employee, conclude the conversation, and walk out.

He was also a very, very funny guy who laughed easily. To him, the world was simply a happy place. He was five foot seven, and we had a running joke about who was taller. Once, in the middle of a big merger, he added a line to the agreement that read, "This issue will be resolved by whoever is taller." No one in the deal ever noticed it. I certainly didn't. I wouldn't have had a clue where to look. In fact, I never read one agreement. Bob, on the other hand, read every document, every word.

Bob was often the instigator of practical jokes in the office. One of his favorite targets was our young accountant, Art Greenberg. Art was a very serious and straitlaced person, so it was fun to tease him. One year, at bonus time, we gave Art a $5,000 cash bonus. Bob put it all in a locked briefcase and handed it to him. Without the combination.

Every once in a while, we couldn't contain our antics within the walls of our offices. One of our first employees was Eileen Blomquist, and among her many skills, she was an artist who created life-size, stuffed likenesses of people. She did a dummy model of Bob, and we would prop it up in his office chair when he was out for long periods of time. At my request, she also created a model of Jim Harper, our lead banker at Continental Bank, which was the primary lender for many of our transactions in the 1970s. On Jim's birthday one year we arranged to have him out of the office, and then we put his stuffed likeness in his chair. I planned to be there to witness the scene when Jim got back so I could see his reaction. But I was delayed. When I finally walked into his office, his dummy was sitting there, holding a pen and leaning over a piece of paper on the desk. I walked up for a closer look and written on the paper were two words, "Pay up." So Jim got the last laugh.

In the beginning, we took nearly all of our returns in residuals, and we charged very little in fees. Eventually, the residual equity turned to cash, and then we'd reinvest it in the business. Consequently, we never had any money. *Never.* We were asset rich and cash poor. We operated the company on a shoestring. One year, we sold the last piece of an asset, got a windfall of $30,000, and promptly bought a stereo system for the office.

We bought a lot of real estate in the seventies, and many of those buildings came from Arthur Cohen, the CEO of Arlen Realty in New York. I was introduced to Arthur in 1974. Four years earlier, he had been on the front cover of *Fortune* magazine as the CEO of the largest real estate company in the world. He was incredibly smart, numerically focused, and a brilliant dealmaker who had zero interest in operations. The result was that he'd make all these brilliant deals, and then they'd inevitably get messed up. He was always leveraging his properties beyond their ability to perform. I think he understood this, but was effectively kicking the can down the road until there was another opportunity in the next market crisis to renegotiate his loans. Arlen Realty had acquired an off-shore real estate mutual fund that created the classic conundrum of investing in long-term assets while offering investors daily re-demption. When the market inevitably softened, those redemp-tions put enormous pressure on Arlen Realty for cash.

When I met Arthur, I was amazed at the complexity of his world. I had never seen anyone handle as many multiple transac-tions with such energy and finesse. But he was going from deal to deal, just putting out fires. His need for cash was both significant and immediate. The fact that Bob and I had dry powder and could make quick decisions positioned us well to cut deals with Arthur. It was my introduction to the value of speed and certainty, and we would eventually gain a reputation for this powerful combination in winning deals—even when we weren't offering the highest price.

So Bob and I stepped in to restructure and acquire various buildings in Arlen Realty's portfolio, and along the way, to pro-vide advice on others. For about four years, I'd have breakfast nearly every Tuesday morning with Arthur at his apartment at Olympia Center in New York to review the deals we were unrav-eling and buying. The experience went a long way in shaping how I would think about real estate for years to come. Among my most salient takeaways was the value of optionality. Arthur was the king of optionality. Quite often, the longer he could wait to commit, the longer he could retain the power of free will.

I was on a good run. Until 1976. A few years earlier, we had acquired a high-rise hotel and apartment complex in Reno. Negotiations had gone on for over a year, and the sticking point had been the substantial gap between the price I was willing to pay and the price at which the owner was willing to sell, on an after-tax basis. He had said, "Look, I've done the numbers, and it isn't worth it to me because the tax bill is so high."

I was determined to figure out a way to make it work, so I took the deal to the law firm where my brother-in-law, Roger, was a principal. Roger, a Harvard-trained lawyer with an impeccable reputation, was my go-to person on real estate deals with tax implications. One of his colleagues, another principal at the firm, crafted a convoluted tax structure for the sale, and Roger served as the scribe. I thought the deal was smart; it never occurred to me that it might not be kosher. We closed it and everyone was satisfied.

Then a couple years later, unbeknownst to me, Roger's law firm, and in particular the architect of my Reno deal, became the target of a broad IRS investigation. My deal got wrapped up in a whole series of unrelated things that the IRS was pursuing with the law firm. The inquiry lasted a year and a half. In 1976, it turned into an investigation. I was "invited" to Reno and told that the IRS had a grand jury convened.

The IRS investigator I met with in Reno asked me what I was going to say to the grand jury. I explained to him how the deal had unfolded. He gave me a hard look and essentially said, "If you don't help us bury this guy [Roger's partner], we're not going to give you a pass."

I'll never forget sitting there. It was around five o'clock at night and getting dark. A very lonely feeling. But I turned to the IRS investigator and said, "Look, I told you the truth. I'm not going to lie or create a story for you. I am simply a deal guy who relied on his tax attorneys."

He responded, "Well, then, we're going to indict you." And

they did. They indicted me and three lawyers from the firm, including Roger.

I hired my own lawyers, and the pressure the IRS put on me in Reno changed once they were dealing with my attorneys rather than just a young real estate guy. They basically said, "You take the stand and tell the truth, and then at the end of the trial we'll dismiss you." And that is exactly what happened.

I sat in the courtroom to support Roger. I didn't know how it would go down, but I remember the faces of the jurors as the evidence was laid out. They seemed to be siding with the government, and I became increasingly convinced that they'd make someone pay. The question was who—and how much? I was relieved to be out of the hot seat personally, but my family and I were worried sick about Roger. When the verdict came in, it was the worst news possible. The attorney that the IRS was originally after—the architect of the deal—was acquitted. Roger, who penned the documents, was convicted. It didn't feel like justice. We pulled together, got through it and past it, and Roger and I continue to have a strong relationship today. But it was a dark period.

There were still some repercussions for me. It didn't matter that I'd been cleared. The stain on my record was that I'd been *indicted*. The first time it came up was for some financing with Northwestern Mutual Life Insurance Company, which had been my first institutional investor partner back in the 1960s. We had a wonderful relationship. But they had some concerns. They invited my lawyer and me to come in and explain things to them. I remember the exact analogy my lawyer used in describing my indictment: "Sam was standing in the railroad station waiting for the train. The train came in and never stopped, and sucked everybody along underneath the tracks." Northwestern checked it out and went ahead with the deal.

The next issue came later that year on another deal, when I

was attempting to buy a distressed asset from a bank. They said they couldn't fund and sell to me because of the indictment. So one of my early investors, Irving Harris, stepped up and back-stopped the deal. That kind of loyalty and trust was very meaningful to me—and was a measure of where I stood with those who knew me. It's easy to support somebody who's hitting home runs. Not so easy to put your reputation at risk and put your name behind someone who is even remotely connected to something nefarious. Time and again I received support like that from those who had done business with me in the past. They *knew* me and how I operated. For me, it all came back to being, in my father's words, a man of *shem tov,* a man of good name.

As the scope of our activities grew, I realized we had to hire an in-house lawyer we could trust completely to oversee all of our matters. I set my sights on Sheli Rosenberg, a young woman who was making a name for herself as a partner at a white-shoe law firm. Sheli was one of the first women to reach that pinnacle. I figured she had to be pretty tough. But when I went to see her at her buttoned-up office wearing a lime green jumpsuit, she couldn't conceal her horror. She turned me down flat. It didn't help that her husband was against the idea. Our office had a reputation for being raucous. We dressed funny. There was rock music playing. It was a loose environment. He was worried about Sheli's reputation.

I didn't give up though. It took eight months to convince Sheli to come on board, and then she stayed for twenty years. Sheli wasn't a typical lawyer. It turned out she loved doing deals too. Sheli loved the energy and the risk. It was a great fit. Not only was she brilliant, she was also a mensch. She mothered the office and became a mentor to the staff. When people had problems, they went to see her. In many respects, Sheli became the holder of the moral code of the office.

Ultimately we created an in-house law firm, which enabled us to better control the speed and efficiency of our legal work. This team eventually grew to more than thirty attorneys. Later, in the 1990s, when we began monetizing our private portfolio through a series of initial public offerings (IPOs), we disbanded our internal law firm due to potential conflicts.

Shortly after Bob died, about ten years after Sheli started, I made her the CEO. I don't know how many other women CEOs in finance there were at the time, but I'm sure there weren't many.

Integrity isn't just about following the letter of the law. It's about how you treat people, doing business in a fair and above-board way, and of course keeping your word. I can't stand bullies or people who are insulting, sneaky, or passive-aggressive. And when I encounter them, there's often a consequence. One day I got a call from Continental Bank about a recent new commit-ment they'd made for a loan to us. They had discovered that with the new loan, we were going to exceed their legal limit of lending to one party, and they asked if we could lay off one of our existing loans to another bank. I called Tim Callahan, our loan officer at Chemical Bank, and he agreed to provide the funding for one of our other assets. He told Chemical Bank's outside lawyer that he had to get the deal done as soon as possible so it didn't hold up my other deal with Continental.

We began the process and Chemical Bank's lawyer just came out swinging. His behavior was outrageous. He was arrogant, intransigent, slow to respond, and abusive to Sheli, our staff, and me. He seemed more focused on running up his legal fees than on actually closing the deal.

Prior to his involvement, the loan that Chemical Bank was going to buy had closed with Continental Bank just sixty days earlier. We had walked through all of the title work and other terms with Tim, and he had approved. But the new lawyer demanded that all the documentation be repeated. Sheli, who could manage anyone, came to me and said, "This guy is just impossible." My response was that unfortunately we had to accept his abuse because we had to close.

We'd finally completed all the documents when we received a demand from the lawyer that his bill be paid before actual closing. In essence, he was holding the closing hostage. It was one step too far and we refused. The deal closed anyway.

Three weeks later, I got a call from one of our internal accounting people reviewing the loan documents. He was calculating the interest rate, which was a complex formula, and determined the rate was at prime, not at one point over prime, which I had agreed to pay Chemical.

So I called Tim and said, "There's a mistake in the documents, and I want to fix it. I agreed to one point over prime and that's what I'll pay. But I want you to picture the following scenario: Two parties agree to a deal and draw up documents. Then Party A hires a lawyer who insists on rewriting the already-approved documents, puts Party B through hell, is abusive and arrogant, and stalls closing. Then Party B discovers this troublesome lawyer has screwed up the documents he insisted on redoing by writing in language detrimental to his own client. Party B, of course, does the right thing and tells his deal partner about it, and reconfirms the previously agreed-upon rate. But now I want your help with something in return."

I asked Tim to call his lawyer and tell him Chemical Bank had discovered the mistake and that he needed to fix it ASAP. So the lawyer called Sheli, said there was a slight problem, a typographical error, and he'd send over an amendment for me to sign.

Sheli, who was prepared for the call, said, "I don't know. Sam was off the wall with how you handled the deal and the way you treated his people. I don't know if he'll be willing to sign, but I'll try."

The lawyer was furious. "That's ridiculous! Of course he'll sign."

He sent over the amendment and we sat on it.

After a week, the lawyer called Sheli. She said, "I tried, but Sam was apoplectic. He won't sign."

The lawyer couldn't believe it. "Impossible. Tell him he has to."

I then called Tim at Chemical and asked him to call the lawyer and inquire where the amendment was. And he did.

So the lawyer called Sheli again. All of a sudden he was conciliatory. He started pleading professional courtesy and asking for cooperation.

We let another week go by, and then Tim called to ask me a hypothetical question. "Say there is man on a scaffold with his head in a noose. How soon after the trapdoor opens do you cut the rope?"

I laughed—and I got his point. It was time to stop the lawyer's squirming. I said, "Okay. But I'd like to do one more thing."

Sheli called the lawyer and told him, "Sam has agreed to sign the amendment subject to two conditions: a waiver of your legal fees and an apology for your behavior on your law firm's stationery." He acquiesced and delivered.

Three weeks later, a senior partner of the lawyer's firm asked to come see me. We had breakfast and he explained that his guy had written the fee waiver without authority, and that kind of written mea culpa simply couldn't exist from a law firm.

I promised I wouldn't share a copy of the letter, and I never did. But it gave me a good story.

CHAPTER FOUR

Grave Dancer

We were having fun, and we were doing extremely well. I realized that the basics of business are straightforward. It's largely about risk. If you've got a big downside and a small upside, run the other way. If you've got a big upside and a small downside, do the deal. Always make sure you're getting paid for the risk you take, and never risk what you cannot afford to lose. Keep it simple. A scenario that takes four steps instead of one means there are three additional opportunities to fail.

I often went back—and still do—to what was written up there on the blackboard when I first walked into Econ 101: Supply and Demand. In fact, much of my career has been about understanding and acting on this basic tenet—whether it's in real estate, oil and gas, manufacturing, or whatever. Opportunity is very often embedded in the imbalance between supply and demand. It could be rising demand against flat or diminishing supply, or flat demand against shrinking supply.

When there's an imbalance, I look at where the two lines will intersect and then determine whether it is cheaper to buy or to build. Usually the answer is in acquisition, which eliminates a lot of the risk inherent in development. I like to invest below replacement cost, thereby creating a competitive advantage.

My commitment to the fundamentals of supply and demand is what inadvertently led to my nickname, the Grave Dancer. Let me set the stage.

By the early 1970s, my investment thesis, focusing on high-growth, small cities, had run its course. The investment community at large had caught on to the idea, and these cities were drawing new competing capital for assets, thereby lowering cap rates (the rate of return based on expected income) and making real estate in these markets more expensive. In response, for a short time, I shifted from buying existing assets to financing new property development. Different than serving as a developer who assumes all the risk for a project, I fed the equity step-by-step, based on measurable milestones.

Before a developer put a shovel in the ground, I became his partner. I took control of the property by agreeing to pay him a determined amount over the mortgage once construction was complete. I paid a portion at the beginning, a portion upon completion, and a portion when the developer achieved roughly 80 percent occupancy. I structured the deals to create the maximum tax considerations, which then subsidized my ownership of the residual and we achieved solid returns.

By 1973, I was starting to realize that the supply-and-demand equilibrium of commercial real estate was getting way out of whack. The harbinger for me was our apartment building, Capistrano, in Orlando, Florida. It was an absolutely beautiful lakefront project. We had completed it in 1971, and within one year it was fully occupied. But by mid-1973, there were six other apartment buildings under construction around the property. Disney World was planning to expand, and the growth projections for multifamily units in the area were astronomical. I realized then it didn't matter if we had the best project. There was simply too much supply. Deep discounts on space, and therefore rents, were inevitable, and we were going to suffer along with everyone else. I turned to the rest of the country to test this logic, and sure enough, I saw the same scenario playing out in cities all over the U.S. The real estate industry was in a building frenzy, and the sky was the limit. It wasn't going to end well.

The market was starting to show the impact of a significant amount of new money that had come into the industry earlier that decade. First, there were dedicated real estate lenders. Each bank or insurance company would start the year with a set amount of lending capital, say $5 billion, to invest. The branch would allocate a certain amount to bonds, a certain amount to equities, and a certain amount to real estate. The rule was that at the end of the year, if each department hadn't invested its full allocation, the capital had to be returned to the parent company. Not surprisingly, the departments never gave anything back. So lenders in the 1970s were often making loans at face rates significantly less than inflation. They justified this based on market share and maintaining staff. Classic institutional, bureaucratic mentality.

Other new money had also flooded the industry from the early real estate investment trusts (REITs). In 1969, Jim Harper had come up with the idea of using the REIT structure to provide financing for short-term commercial construction loans. As a result, the construction REIT industry went from $1 billion to $21 billion within three years, fueling massive real estate development. Institutions were creating REITs like crazy. It was all easy money with no consideration of risk, hung on the premise that the industry could create demand rather than respond to it. The results were predictable. Oversupply led to losses, and the $21 billion REIT market plummeted to $11 billion in just two years.

This has always been a fatal flaw in U.S. real estate: the volume of development has been related to the availability of funds, not to demand. The industry has a long history of overbuilding when there's easy money, without regard for who will occupy those spaces once they're built.

At the same time that construction cranes were dotting the horizon of every major city, the country was just starting to tip into a recession. Supply was going up and prospects for demand were not good. I was certain that we were headed toward a massive oversupply and a crash was coming.

That's when I just said, "Stop." I was done.

I stopped buying assets, started accumulating capital, and got ready for what I was sure would be the greatest buying opportunity of my career thus far. My thesis was that over the next five years, we would have the opportunity to make a fortune by acquiring distressed real estate. So I established a property management firm, First Property Management Company (FPM), to focus on distressed assets.

Everyone thought I was nuts. After all, occupancies were still over 90 percent. Absorption was high. Companies were hiring. It was one of many times I would hear people tell me that I just didn't understand.

I didn't listen. I just stepped aside while the music was still playing. It was the biggest risk I had taken to date in my career. After all, I had a stable of investors by then. What would they think if I bowed out and the end *didn't* come? That would mean

I was forgoing a lot of upside for them. It was a true test of my conviction. But I had to follow the logic of supply and demand.

Turns out I was right. Less than one year later, in 1974, the market crashed. Hard. Overnight, we were buying assets at 50 cents on the dollar.

At the time, financial institutions did not have to mark to market. In other words, they didn't have to adjust the book value of their assets to the current market value those assets could actually sell for. If you were an insurance company, instead of marking to market, you could avoid taking a hit to your books if you determined that by restructuring the deal you could get back to par within five years. So I'd come in and offer the solution to their problems. To me, that is the essence of being an entrepreneur—to not just recognize problems but to provide solutions.

I looked at each property and figured out how much debt service it could handle based on its existing cash flow. I'd restructure the debt at a lower interest rate and put $1 down on the property along with a limited cash-flow guarantee to ensure the institution would not go into default while waiting for the market to recover.

For example, if it was an apartment building with a 7 percent loan for ten years, but the asset could only service debt at 4 percent, my guarantee assured the lender that the restructured loan would not default during the period of the guarantee. I put up virtually no capital, just a limited guarantee that I'd feed the deficit of the loan if necessary to keep it current over a three-year period, which was how long I thought it would take for the market's supply/demand equilibrium to return. It worked because the lenders' only alternative was to take back the assets, which meant taking over management—something they did not want to do. They had no structure in place to manage all those buildings.

We did. We were ready. There was so much supply and opportunity we branched out from apartments into retail and office buildings. Between 1974 and 1977, we bought roughly $4 billion in assets with $1 down and a hope certificate.

In general, the buildings I chose had a few common denominators. First, they had to be available below replacement cost. If I could set rents based on a $10,000-per-unit purchase price, and the sunk costs of new development were $20,000 per unit, a new building would be priced out of the market.

Second, they had to be good-quality, well-located properties, which usually perform better than market throughout economic cycles. Tenants tend to stick in the up cycle, and upgrade to nicer space in the down cycle as rental rates fall. So better assets provided more stable cash flow, and that gave us downside protection.

Many of the properties I chose also had deferred maintenance. While the structures were good, repairs and upgrades had been neglected. So there was room for improvements that would help us lease more space, often at higher rents, thereby improving the value of the asset.

To manage so many properties effectively and with the care needed to protect and enhance their value, I knew the management had to be done in-house. That's where FPM, our new distressed property management company, came in. We brought our $4 billion of newly acquired assets—apartments, office buildings, shopping centers, hotels, and so on—right into FPM.

The 1970s could have been a disaster for us. They were for many in real estate. Instead, they were a great ride. Our firm ended the decade with an enormous, diverse portfolio, some of which would later seed two of the largest REITs in the industry.

Years later, people would ask me, "How did you know when and what to buy?" But all I basically did was create a massive arbitrage—a fixed-rate instrument in an inflationary environment. I essentially took on $4 billion of nonrecourse debt at an average interest rate of 6 percent in an environment with inflation of 9 percent or higher. That means I was already making 3 percent returns the second the deal closed—without doing a thing to the assets. Sure, we picked some terrific properties, but every one didn't have to be Class A. Overall, it was the creation of an enormous amount of nonrecourse, fixed-rate debt (in some cases three to four hundred basis points, or 3 to 4 percent) below inflation. When we started, my estimate was that we could make $50 million (equivalent to about $250 million today) in five years. What I didn't envision was that the country would elect Jimmy Carter. As a result, everything he did raised inflation. So we made a lot more.

During this period, I wrote an article for *Real Estate Review* called "The Grave Dancer." My use of the moniker in the title was meant somewhat facetiously and probably inaccurately. I wasn't so much dancing on graves as I was raising the dead. As I wrote:

> A review of the current list of bestselling fiction reveals a novel that needs to be written. Titled *The Grave Dancer*, it would be a story of an individual or organization immersed in resurrecting the real estate corpses created by the greatest explosion of real estate lending and building in the country's history. Somehow, Arthur Haley and Harold Robbins have both missed this great idea for a bestseller containing all the excitement and intrigue of their other chronicles.

This bit of hyperbole revealed a very important fact: At its heart, grave dancing was an opportunity to resurrect those assets deserving of a fresh start. It was a bet on my ability to affect a turnaround. And the low entry price paid for the risk I was taking to do it.

Grave dancing involves confidence, optimism, conviction, and no small amount of courage. All the opportunity in the world means nothing if you don't actually pull the trigger.

One of my favorite parables is about a man named Moishe. He was an observant Jew who owned an appliance store in Brooklyn. For years Moishe was very successful, but then people started moving out of the neighborhood, and soon his business was struggling. So one Saturday at temple, Moishe prayed for help. "God, I've never asked you for anything, and I've always been very devout. But I've got a problem. My business is dying. God, I need to win the lottery."

The next morning, Moishe checked the lottery results in the newspaper and saw that he hadn't won. The following Saturday, he again went to temple; things were worse than ever, and he prayed even more fervently. "God," he prayed, "things are getting bad. My creditors are calling every day. Please, I've never asked you for anything before, but I really need to win the lottery."

Again, the following morning, Moishe checked the lottery results in the newspaper and again he hadn't won. By the third Saturday, he was desperate. At temple, he again prayed, "God, I've *got* to win the lottery!" Then from on high came the voice of God: "Moishe . . . You've got to buy a ticket!" The moral of the story of course is that it's hard to get a hit if you don't step up to bat.

Grave Dancer

• • •

By the mid-1970s, we had gained enough of a reputation that at the end of each year, we were inundated with gifts from people we had either done business with or who wanted to do business with us. I got calendars, pens, and a ridiculous number of key chains. I felt we had to reciprocate, but I just couldn't see putting our name on throwaway stuff like that. I wanted to send something with more depth. Something that told people where our heads were at and how we viewed the market. So I created a simple Lucite block engraved with "We Suffer From Knowing the Numbers." It relayed our frustration with a fundamental truth. We loved doing deals, but we weren't deal junkies. The ultimate discipline was that we were always committing our own money. We weren't going to sacrifice the outcome when the numbers said turn the other way. The building boom in the first half of the decade had been intoxicating, yet we had stayed home from the party. But "knowing the numbers" means having the discipline to listen to them—even if they're not telling you what you want to hear. Some of the best deals, of course, are the ones you don't do.

I ended my 1976 article, "The Grave Dancer," with an important warning: "Grave dancing is an art that has many potential benefits. But one must be careful while prancing around not to fall into the open pit and join the cadaver. There is often a thin line between the dancer and the danced upon."

Vigilance was essential—as the 1980s would prove. In 1984, eight years after that article, I wrote "The Return of the Grave Dancer" for the same publication. Times had changed. As I wrote, "Like Rip Van Winkle, the Grave Dancer hibernates from one real estate cycle to the next."

Sure enough, in the mid-1980s, we were beginning to see an orgy of development that was even more extensive and more threatening to the overall real estate market than we'd encountered a decade earlier. Once again, there was excess availability of capital creating oversupply with total disregard for demand. Initially the incentives made real estate, relatively speaking, more attractive, but the industry's lack of discipline would be, yet again, its downfall.

And once again, we saw it coming and our foresight would be a game changer for us. In 1980, Bob and I sat down and listed the reasons we didn't like where the real estate market was headed. First, the key to our prior success had been an inefficient market. The real estate industry had always been fragmented, with valuations and projections that often varied widely. That started changing rapidly with the debut of Hewlett-Packard's financial calculator. All of a sudden, any owner could hire an MBA with an HP-12C to run ten years of cash flows, none of which considered recessions or rent dips, and make an elaborate and sophisticated case for investment—and a bunch of eager investors would show up to check out the property. That was not an arena we wanted to compete in. Second, up until then, lenders made long-term, fixed-rate, nonrecourse loans. But as a result of inflation in the 1970s, they got scared and switched to short-term, floating-rate loans. We believed the real money in real estate came from borrowing long-term, fixed-rate debt in an inflationary scenario that ultimately depreciated the value of the loan and increased the position of the borrower. Finally, we had always looked at the tax benefits of real estate as what you got for the lack of liquidity. All of a sudden, sellers were including a value for tax benefits in their asset pricing.

So we said, "If we've been as successful in real estate as we have been, aren't we really just good businessmen? And if we're good businessmen, then why wouldn't the same principles that apply to buying real estate apply to buying anything else?" We checked the boxes—supply and demand, barriers to entry, tax considerations—all of the criteria that governed our decisions in real estate, and didn't see any differences. So we set a goal that we would diversify our investment portfolio to be 50 percent real estate and 50 percent *non*-real estate by 1990.

We narrowed our universe by targeting good asset-intensive companies with bad balance sheets, a thesis similar to real estate. We liked asset-intensive investments because if the world ended, there would be something to liquidate. The low-tech manufacturing and agricultural chemical industries were perfect fits for us—the former driven by Bob with his expertise in engineering and passion for anything mechanical.

It was a big change, and it coincided with another new adventure in my life at the time—my second marriage, to Sharon, in June 1979. Janet and I had divorced four years earlier, and maintained a relationship, sharing our kids and eventually our grandkids.

I met Sharon on a blind date by way of a friend and business associate who was convinced we'd do well together. Sharon was a beauty queen—Miss USA, actually—from Louisiana. We clicked instantly. At dinner when I learned that we both enjoyed doing crossword puzzles, I told her that I had the Sunday *New York Times* puzzle in my hotel room and asked her if she wanted to come back with me to do it. She misconstrued my meaning. But that really was exactly what I meant. So we ended up by the hotel's outdoor pool at 11:00 p.m. that night doing the crossword. We began dating seriously and were married a few years later. I worked hard to win over her eleven-year-old daughter, Kellie, from a previous marriage, and after she and Sharon moved to Chicago, I would take Kellie to school on the back of my motorcycle. I had the honor of adopting her on her eighteenth birthday.

Going back to the business, Bob's and my decision to expand from solely real estate to include "corporate" investments was facilitated by a weakening U.S. economy, which created an environment of disruption that was perfectly suited for us as opportunistic investors. Weak economies breed troubled companies, and we knew there would be significant opportunities as overleveraged companies would be forced to restructure. The assets they would jettison at attractive prices were our targets of opportunity. The hardest-hit industries were manufacturing, construction, and automotive.

Around the same time, Congress passed the Economic Recovery Tax Act. Among other things, it extended the life of net operating loss carry-forwards (NOLs) from seven to fifteen years. NOLs allow companies to offset their current year's taxable income with past losses, thereby reducing current tax liability. The goal of the act was to help struggling companies recover and to enable their shareholders to benefit from the prior losses.

We took a look at all of the public companies with large NOLs and found something surprising. These companies had virtually no change in share price as a result of the new legislation. The market was overlooking the significant value added through the extended life of NOLs. That presented us with an enormous opportunity to gain control of those NOLs and create holding companies for businesses whose profits would be shielded. If a company was trading at $3 a share for a total enterprise value of $45 million and it had $350 million in NOLs, we knew we could create profits that were sheltered and convert those NOLs (which were valued at $0) to roughly $100 million of cash, or 25 cents on the dollar over time. And that's just what we did. Our strategy became: Find the NOLs, add profitable business subsidiaries, and, ultimately, maximize the value of an asset we didn't pay anything for in the first place. The NOLs would also lower the risk of our investment. The goal, however, was to use the advantage to build companies, not just monetize the NOLs. They created the opportunity for significant capital gains and offered a new twist on grave dancing.

Ironically, the first NOL company we found to serve as a holding company for our manufacturing business acquisitions had its origins in real estate. Great American Management and Investment Corp. (GAMI) was once the sixth largest REIT in the country. It had provided construction loans secured by mortgages until it became overleveraged in the 1973 recession.

GAMI had $130 million in NOLs on its books, as well as a significant number of foreclosed hotels and apartments. We sold those assets and to maximize the sales prices we provided financing to the buyers. This also gave us a significant pool of loan receivables, which we then used as collateral to finance our acquisitions of profitable companies.

At the time, banks were limited in the amount of equity they took as collateral, so they had to hold a higher level of reserves. Equity carried on our balance sheet provided a very small borrowing base. On the other hand, when we used loan receivables as collateral with banks, we could dramatically increase the amount of capital they'd lend us. As a huge consumer of capital, I have always made it a mission to understand lenders' motivations and the methodologies behind their credit structures.

Our largest subsidiary under GAMI was Eagle Industries, which was a collection of dull-tech (as opposed to high-tech) companies, like air conditioner manufacturers. We acquired the companies one at a time as we achieved scale. And we used the

NOLs to shelter income from taxes, turning GAMI into a diversified holding company.

If you're wondering whether others were following the same strategy, they weren't. NOLs were extremely challenging, and subject to complex and arcane rules that you had to learn. That may seem contrary to my belief in simplicity, but it eliminated the competition. By their nature, NOLs served as a barrier to entry. Most other deal makers couldn't stomach the rigor of mastering NOL rules, so there were very few other buyers.

Frankly, there's no substitute for limited competition. You can be a genius, but if there's a lot of competition, it won't matter. I've spent my career trying to avoid its destructive consequences. Competition skews people's assessments; as buyers get competitive, the demand for assets inflates pricing, often beyond reason.

I jokingly tell people that competition is great—for *you*. Me, I'd rather have a natural monopoly, and if I can't get that, I'll take an oligopoly.

Not long after we got involved with GAMI, we found another NOL opportunity in Itel, a conglomerate founded in 1967 as a computer leasing company. Itel had expanded into leasing aircraft, railcars, and shipping containers. Throughout the 1970s, it was a giant and flamboyant company, known for its corporate excess. The management threw lavish parties, filled the drinking fountains at headquarters with Perrier, installed Persian rugs in the executive offices, and gave massive bonuses to senior executives. Even while the company was struggling, it sent its sales staff on a $1.5 million Caribbean cruise.

In 1981, Itel was one of the largest bankruptcies in the history of the country. It emerged from Chapter 11 in 1983 with its container-leasing and railcar-leasing businesses at its core, $450 million in NOLs, and a break-even cash flow.

That's when we got interested. We started buying stock at $3 a share. When we had accumulated a 5 percent ownership stake in the company, I went to meet with the board and requested a seat at the table. They politely declined. Being no stranger to rejection, I parted amicably and continued to buy stock, increasing our ownership to 22 percent. This led to a reconsideration by the board, and in April 1985, I was elected chairman and CEO. Up to that point the company had been run by a trustee from the bankruptcy days who then became the CEO. He was about eighty years old, worked a couple of days a week, and wasn't exactly engaged. He passed the torch to me at the annual shareholders' meeting. There were about three hundred people there. As I surveyed the crowded room, I couldn't help noticing that the mood was hostile. The shareholders seemed pissed off and suspicious. They had heard the promises and hype about growth potential from too many people too many times. I got up and talked about how we were going to transform the company—that we were going to make acquisitions and that we were going to take advantage of the NOLs and grow.

A guy popped up in the crowd. "Excuse me," he said, "but the previous management constantly talked about acquisitions and they never did anything. How close are you to actually getting something done?"

How to answer? The difference, of course, was that I wasn't just a manager. I was an owner, an *active* owner. But in the tone of his question I could hear all of the pent-up frustration in the room. I wasn't prepared to talk about specifics, even though I already had a deal in the works, but it was important to let them know this was not the same old routine they'd been fed before. So, as I'm apt to do, I chose a metaphor to convey my point. "I'd like you to picture the following scene," I said. "You're sitting at a great restaurant at a table with a white tablecloth and candle-light. There's a beautiful woman sitting across from you. You've just finished a wonderful dinner with excellent wine, and you're sipping a glass of port. The music is softly playing in the background. The two of you look deep into each other's eyes. And my question to you is: 'How close are you?'"

The room cracked up, and all the tension went out of the place. I managed to defuse their anger, if not quite win their trust. But I knew I'd have to act fast to back it up.

Itel had three divisions: freight containers, railcars, and miscellaneous. In the miscellaneous category was a hodgepodge of orphaned equipment and leasing contracts. Since we needed capital, the first goal was to liquidate all the miscellaneous stuff. We did, for about $50 million.

The oceangoing freight container leasing industry was an oligopoly of about seven providers. Itel was number four. We bought number three, and then we bought number seven and became number one. Our strategy was simple. Let's say Itel had revenues of $100 million and expenses of $50 million. And number three had revenues of $100 million and expenses of $50 million. Each company had its own extensive operating and logistics system—separate facilities in each city, separate computer systems, and so on. By eliminating the redundancies, we increased margins by 20 percent.

This was my first experience listening to proposals about the great "synergies" of mergers. As an investor and a risk taker, my focus has to be on what is specifically attainable. Buying another company based on the perception of opportunities for cross-selling and other intangible benefits generally represents a much higher level of risk than I believe is justified. Therefore, I concentrate on eliminating redundancies, which measurably reduces the capital required to run the business. This epiphany later became relevant across industries from drugstores, to radio stations, to supermarkets, and others. Redundancies are much more predictable and transparent than theoretical opportunities to add value. My focus is always on the downside. Overly optimistic assumptions lead to the graveyard of corporate acquisitions.

Finally, we looked at the railcar business and tried to understand where it was going to go. At that time, owning railcars was considered about the worst thing you could do. I said, "Let's look at the numbers." We did, and there was the opportunity based on—you guessed it—supply and demand.

In a single year, 1979, the industry had built over 100,000 railcars. Like real estate earlier that decade, the railcar industry had succumbed to easy money and tax incentives for building, and disregarded the realities of demand. That bubble burst in 1981, and over the next five years the industry built only 20,000 railcars total. During that same period, 65 percent of the existing railcars in the country were scrapped. On the demand side, loadings were flat but stable.

I don't think you need a degree from MIT to follow the two lines: demand was flat, supply was going down. At some point, those two lines were going to intersect, and when they did, anybody with railcars was going to make a lot of money. At the same time, the average utilization of our Itel fleet was only 32 percent due to lack of demand. Across the industry, the average utilization rate for older cars was even lower, so scrappage was increasing. It seemed to me that the logical strategy was to buy up all the used railcars in America. So we did.

Buying railcars in the mid-1980s was like buying apartment buildings in the mid-1970s. Railcars were available at half or less the cost to create them (replacement cost). The thesis of our consolidation was that not only would the supply/demand lines cross but that by owning a fleet with a cost basis of half the competitions', we would have a competitive advantage and produce superior results. Everybody thought we were nuts. But it worked. I don't know why no one else saw the opportunity. I only know we had conviction in our view of the market, and we believed it enough to invest real money behind it.

One of our Itel transactions in 1988 included the Pullman Company, one of the largest assemblages of grain and tank railcars in the country. In order to make the deal work, we had to acquire the seller's 17 percent interest in Santa Fe Southern Pacific Corporation, and that meant a seat for me on that company's board.

It's hard to imagine someone like me being added to a board that had been reconstituted through the 1983 merger of Santa Fe and Southern Pacific and included directors of both companies. There were thirty directors. *Thirty!* At the time, boards like this were populated by people with good resumes who were often past their prime. Picture row upon row of conservative older white guys in dark suits. To say the least, when I'd show up for a board meeting with my motorcycle helmet under my arm, it created a significant contrast between me and the establishment.

My first board meeting for Santa Fe was awful. I went in with the commitment to myself that, as the new guy, I would keep quiet at the first meeting, and although I accomplished that objective, it was excruciating. The first order of business was an executive session in which the head of human resources delivered a booklet outlining the succession plan in case of a catastrophic event that resulted in the death of executives. Oddly enough, the same individual was named as the successor for each executive position.

The next order of business was a thirty-minute monologue by the CEO, during and after which no one asked a single question. Meanwhile, a dozen other company executives sat along the wall ready for their ten minutes each. By the time the third executive started droning on, two of the board members were sound asleep. And still no one in the room had asked a question. It struck me that most of the directors were more interested in the two-day event's lunch and dinner menus than they were in what was going on in the company. It depressed the hell out of me.

After that first meeting, I was very vocal, often serving as a lone voice on strategy amid a steady stream of irrelevant reporting on minutiae. The ultimate example occurred in one meeting when the head of the railroad, after going through the forecasts, mentioned as a last item that his capital expense budget for the following year was $250 million. Then the CEO started to transition to the next business head.

"Excuse me," I said. "Can we back up a minute? I have a question. What's the rate of return you expect on that $250 million of cap ex?"

He stared at me, perplexed. "I don't understand your question," he said, clearly not used to being queried. "We have to run the railroad. We have to fix the tracks, and that's what it's going to cost."

I replied, "But capital expenditures should be related to profitability and return on investment. And if you're spending money on tracks that aren't profitable, that's not a good business decision." The head of the railroad and the CEO just sat there and stared at me like I had two heads, unable to comprehend this basic concept. Then they moved on without answering my question.

The experience was shocking. I realized then the danger of

boards that were beset by cronyism and inertia—as if an appointment to a board was a perk, a retirement benefit or a no-strings gift to golfing buddies. My philosophy on board composition and culture is the antithesis of what I saw on the Santa Fe board. As the chairman of public companies, I've always selected board members based on the assumption that they were cheap consultants to the business, not potted plants. I've never hesitated to use them—or to have management teams use them—to further the objectives of the company. Also, board materials are prepared with all relevant information prior to meetings. Board members are expected to read the materials in advance, and the real purpose of the meetings is to generate robust discussion. Our board meetings are often raucous, with frequent interruptions, questions, and commentary. As a result, our companies have always benefited from the combined wisdom of our directors.

My experience with Santa Fe also gave me a heightened awareness that companies absolutely need engaged owners. It's an owner who is willing to give up short-term benefits for long-term gains. It's an owner who uses vision to steward a company and guide management. And it's an owner who brings in resources—additional capital, financial expertise, banking relationships, whatever it takes—to help a company and its management team succeed.

My interests have always been and will always be directly aligned with the shareholders of the companies I chair. I've got a stake. I've got skin in the game. Just like I make sure my people have skin in the game in our investments at EGI.

Whether it's in the boardroom or at the management level, I start with this: Don't depend on people unless you understand their motivations and you are confident that your interests align with theirs. Be an owner, act like an owner, and when it comes to your investments, do everything you can to make sure everybody is aligned.

A lot of Wall Street's headaches—the executive compensation issues, the accounting scandals, the options backdating, the subprime mortgage mess—can be chalked up to misaligned interests created when there's too much reliance on outsiders who don't have a stake. Similarly, a lot of people who get burned by depending on Wall Street analysts, or hedge fund managers, or their local stock picker discover quickly that the advice they're getting isn't coming from a committed owner—it's coming from a professional who is collecting a fee. After all, it ain't *their* money.

It has never occurred to me to question whether I should do something simply because I haven't done it before. One of my favorite examples of this was Itel's acquisition of Anixter, a wiring and cable distribution company, in 1987.

Up until then, our investment decisions had been based on buying broken companies on the cheap, below replacement cost, and building them from there. Anixter was completely contrary to this thesis; the company was all about growth, and it wasn't cheap.

In November 1986, I got the call from Merrill Lynch telling me that Alan Anixter wanted to sell his company, Anixter Brothers, at the fixed price of $14 per share, two times the company's book value.

After a hard look, we came to the conclusion that the company's book value was based solely on the hard assets and discounted Anixter's substantial sales and distribution pipeline, which enabled vendors to reach smaller buyers. The pipeline was the most valuable growth asset of the company, but the value didn't appear on the balance sheet. All the company needed was capital and an appetite for risk.

Alan wanted to close the transaction before the end of the year to avoid a scheduled increase in the capital gains tax. I had two weeks to decide if I wanted to play. We were nimble, with the ability to make fast decisions and execute quickly—in fact, we had a reputation for it. So I said, "Let's go."

Our question with Anixter then became "How do we leverage this pipeline?" Itel was a unique entity with which to acquire Anixter. Itel's railcars and containers threw off a large amount of cash flow and depreciation, which would enable us to take the excess cash flow and rapidly expand Anixter across the globe. So in 1991, we decided to focus Itel's business around this small subsidiary. We applied a long-term investment horizon to invest in start-up locations in various countries in Europe, Asia, and Latin America, incurring the inherent start-up costs and operating losses that come with building an overseas network. We had a bigger appetite for risk and were taking it off a much larger base than when Anixter was a family business, since Itel was a conglomerate. When we acquired it, Anixter had $650 million in sales. Today, Anixter's revenue is over $6 billion, and it is one of the largest distributors of communications cabling products in the world. And I'm still chairman of the board and a significant shareholder in the company.

Anixter and its explosive expansion converted Itel into a growth vehicle, and we decided to sell all of the holding company's other subsidiaries. It was the right answer, but getting there was painful. In 1992, I sat down with GE Capital Railcar

Services with a proposal to lease them Itel's entire railcar fleet. The twelve-year lease was for about $150 million per year, with an option to purchase the fleet at the end of the lease period for an additional $500 million. It was an exceedingly complex arrangement, with Itel and GE holding the cars in trust together and GE paying Itel under the terms of the trust. We were dealing with 70,000 railcars, many with debt on them, and hundreds of customer leases. The process was a labyrinth, one of the most excruciating of my career.

GE was a very conservative, patient deal partner, the antithesis of my decisive, efficiency-focused nature. Every time we turned around, there was another problem, another delay, another issue or demand they hadn't raised before. Nine months in, we were nearing a close. But then the bean counters found that the books were off by 2 cents. Everything hit a wall for two weeks while they went back and recalculated the entire transaction until they found the error. For 2 cents. On a $2.3 billion transaction.

Eventually we closed, and it was a great deal for everyone. But I called it the deal from hell because getting there felt like going down into Dante's inferno. In fact, it was such an extraordinary process that I wanted to memorialize it. So I commissioned a painting that depicted the key participants and their roles, along with various scenes over the last year. The final result was a six-by-five-foot oil painting that depicted Dante's (or in our case Itel CFO, Jim Knox's) journey through hell. The ominous warning "Abandon hope all ye who enter here" is scrawled across the bottom of the piece. The painting features a web of players including a bald-headed guy checking his unfurling list; the GE team wielding their shields against risk; the attorneys with hands over their eyes and ears, drowning in paper; and representatives from the IRS, Justice Department, and the Securities and Exchange Commission. I am depicted as *saltator sepulcri*, Latin for "grave dancer," in the form of the persona created for me—a jester. It was a nod to our Eleventh Commandment, "Thou shalt not take thyself too seriously," as well as to my dry sense of humor, sarcasm, and tendency for storytelling and jokes. An accompanying narration of the deal is written in the meter of Dante. Frances Lewis, a co-conspirator on my annual gifts, used clever and sophisticated language to deliver the message.

We sent everyone who worked on the deal a copy of the painting, and it is displayed on the wall in EGI's main entranceway as a reminder of the horrors of hell and our quest for a more "heavenly" (that is, more measured, commonsense, practical, and visionary) approach to deal making.

Around this time, while I was expanding into new industries and unlocking the hidden value of NOLs, I went on my first international motorcycle trip. My friends and I went to Nepal in South Asia. Upon landing in Kathmandu, we learned that it was a national holiday, so hardly anyone was working the day we arrived. We rented motorcycles, and our host led us about twelve kilometers outside of town along a wide river at the base of a mountain range. We pulled over for lunch next to a group of about twenty people sitting on blankets. Most of them turned out to be American expats—conscientious objectors who had renounced their citizenship during the Vietnam War and stayed. They invited us to sit with them, and we did. We were enjoying the sunny day, drinking wine and eating sandwiches, when an old woman carrying a shopping bag down the nearest mountain walked toward us. It was filled with high-quality cannabis, and she offered to sell it to us for $10. So we bought it and shared it enthusiastically with our new friends. At some point the guy I was sitting next to turned to me and asked, "So what do you do?" I replied, "I'm a professional opportunist." And that has been my response to that question ever since.

CHAPTER FIVE

Into the Inferno

I've always believed I am at my best when the scenario around me is at its worst. And I was never tested more than in the early 1990s when I was faced with repeated crises and staggering challenges. The first, in 1990, was the worst of all. I lost Bob.

By then Bob and I had been partners for about twenty years. Our friendship and trust, different perspectives, and opposing banter and laughter defined our business; it was the secret sauce to our success. Losing him was an unthinkable blow personally and professionally. It raised all kinds of questions for me. We had been phenomenally successful. How much of it was Bob? How much of it was Sam? For a time I was caught up in these questions.

Bob was only forty-six in 1987 when he was diagnosed with advanced colon cancer. He didn't tell anyone—even me—for a long time. As he explained to his wife, "I'm not going to be able to stand it if people mourn me before I'm gone." He knew his diagnosis was dire, but he kept coming to the office for two years until the end of 1989, when he was too weak.

I admit that when Bob got sick, I went into irrational denial. I just assumed that he'd get well, and when he wasn't in the office I focused on covering the bases until he was better. We talked two to three times a day, but I didn't go to see him. We had an unspoken understanding that we wanted to interact as if he were fully capable. Seeing his physical deterioration would have impeded our normal discourse. Certainly his mind was as sharp as ever.

Then one Saturday, a couple of months after Bob had stopped coming in, he walked into my office. I was dumbstruck by his appearance—at how frail he was as he lowered himself into a chair and said we had to talk. He looked me straight in the eye and he said, "Sam, you have to understand. I'm going to die, and I'm going to die soon."

It was the first time I really faced the truth. I was devastated. Bob knew I had been in denial, and his visit to my office was his way of bursting that bubble. The impending loss was almost too much to bear. I spoke with him as much as I could during his final months, and I was with him when he died.

Bob's birthday was April 21, and he was always very superstitious about the number 421. It had a weird way of periodically appearing in our lives. On his last night, Bob's wife, Ann, his doctor, and I stayed up with him all night, and we all went silent and shared a moment as we stared at the clock together and it clicked to 4:21. The next morning Bob went to hospice. He died on June 20, 1990. To this day, my plane's tail number is 421 SZ.

A gaping hole opened up in my life when Bob died. In a way, it was also my moment of truth because his death coincided with the most challenging time in our business to date. Just weeks later, the economy had tipped into a full-blown recession. Moreover, the savings and loan crisis and other factors had led to the loss of dedicated real estate lenders, so there was no refinancing for highly leveraged asset owners, including us. We had amassed and were managing a large investment portfolio, in real estate and corporate assets, with about twenty-four hundred employees across the country.

We were rich in assets but starved for cash, and the insatiable need for capital dominated my waking hours. There were weeks when our billion-dollar company was scrambling to scrape up enough money to make payroll. In addition, standard practice in loan documents at the time enabled any bank to call your loan if they felt it was in jeopardy. So if one bank called its loan, it was entirely possible it would create a domino effect and the others would follow. And we were starting to see that happen across the industry.

It was a time of enormous grief and uncertainty. To stave off panic, I drew on an experience that had happened over two decades prior—the first and only time I can remember feeling truly overwhelmed in my career.

It was 1969, and I was young and cocky and doing deals. I was renting an office in a law firm and one of the senior partners introduced me to a guy at Ford Motor Land Development Corporation. The two of us agreed to partner in the development of a 200,000-square-foot office/industrial building. Based on the Ford guy's verbal commitment, I put up a $25,000 deposit for an industrial building—a lot of money to me in 1969—to tie up the deal. Then at the last minute before closing, I got a phone call that Ford Motor Land had reneged, which left me—and my $25,000—twisting in the wind. I was worried about the deposit, sure, but I was also worried about upholding my commitment. It was my first big crisis.

I hung up the phone, jumped up, and ran full out through the law firm halls into the senior partner's office. I was apoplectic. I couldn't talk loud or fast enough.

Well, the partner was one of those guys who was very measured and always spoke evenly and softly. I never saw him lose his temper or his cool. He sat me down and very quietly asked me questions at a regulated pace. As we discussed the alternatives and talked through all the angles, I felt my blood pressure return to normal. And I went and got the deal done with somebody else. That was the day I learned, thanks to that attorney, that a leader can't let his emotions impact his stability. You have to have methods that keep you steady.

I learned to shift some of my reliance and trust from Bob to the team we had built, particularly the strong core senior people in our corporate office. We powered through, and I focused my efforts on leading us through the turmoil.

I'm a prolific maker of lists, and the more trouble I had in the early 1990s, the more I attacked it and dealt with it by making lists and checking off items as we accomplished them. My big-picture goals were all about creating liquidity by monetizing assets, fundraising for opportunities on the horizon, and doing great deals. By zeroing in on the tasks to accomplish each of them, I avoided being overwhelmed, professionally and emotionally.

My first priority was cash. I couldn't jeopardize what we had built by selling in desperation, but I couldn't keep going without cash. I didn't know it then, but this phase in my career was the genesis of a mantra I would repeat regularly for decades to come: *Liquidity equals value.*

The only channel for liquidity was the capital markets. So in 1991, I did my first IPO with Vigoro, a fertilizer company specializing in potash, a potassium compound that is an important nutrient for plants and animals. When we first invested in Vigoro in 1985, we didn't know shit about shit, but the company ticked off all the right boxes. We also had an instinct about Vigoro. We liked the people involved and felt that their priorities were in sync with ours. After meeting with them, it took us less than a day to decide to invest our first $10 million in the company.

I was familiar with the capital markets from our corporate investments. Itel and GAMI were both public when we got involved, but I had never done an IPO. I let the bank run the Vigoro deal, and it drove me nuts. I realized that I didn't know enough to be able to protect myself, and that meant I was displacing—and increasing—the risk. Further, as a huge perpetual consumer of capital, I respected the fact that there is no more consistent source of capital than the public markets.

So I went to school, so to speak, and I learned everything there was about doing offerings. Eventually, I got to the point where I'd run the book on my IPOs. I'd manage the process, and on some deals I'd be up until three in the morning the day of closing, allocating stock to the various players. That meant I had to learn who all the players were, including which ones had a track record of being real investors rather than flippers. I created personal relationships with the buyers, demonstrating my engagement and commitment to being a long-term owner. And I got particularly good at the road shows, eventually doing hundreds of IPO presentations for our various companies all over the world.

Attracting investors is as much art as science. To gain an advantage, I get creative. These guys see ten presentations a day. They are inundated with seemingly great companies to invest in. To them, I am just another face in the succession. I have just forty-five minutes to make a pitch, answer questions, and leave an impression, so I create custom T-shirts to help seal the deals.

I gained a reputation for doing IPO road show T-shirts with memorable, often tongue-in-cheek, spins. They are the calling cards of our sponsorship. And while I didn't do the road show for Vigoro, I did commemorate the deal with green T-shirts that read: "People Shoot It, Spread It, Sling It, Step in It and Let It Happen . . . We Make Money with It."

Vigoro became a successful public company, and when we exited in 1996, the asset had delivered more than a 900 percent return on its original equity.

I used the same approach for our roadshows in fund-raising, and in 1990 we took that to a whole new level. As I've said, at the time I was targeting good real estate assets overburdened by excessive debt. Well, I began seeing similar scenarios unfold in the corporate world and realized I could provide equity to those companies for a stake at a discounted price, and that would help them position themselves for when the market recovered. So I teamed up with Chilmark Partners to form a $1 billion distressed opportunity fund. David Schulte, head of Chilmark, and I made more than two hundred personal sales calls in seven months—in over a dozen countries. We crisscrossed the globe, explaining our idea and pitching investors on the notion that we could find good companies with bad balance sheets and help them grow out of their troubles.

It was a wild ride. On one trip we had to be in Vienna in the morning, Basel for dinner, and Paris the following morning for breakfast. We couldn't make it work with commercial flights, so we chartered a plane. But we were grounded by weather, and so the two of us found ourselves in a three-person sleeping car on the train from Basel to Paris in the middle of the night, perched on two tiny bunk beds, trying to sleep. I was worried about the third guy who was sharing our sleeping car, so I slept all night clutching my briefcase.

Meetings blurred. Sometimes we couldn't remember who we were talking to, or whether we were repeating ourselves. It was a road show like no other. But by the end, we had raised over $1 billion. I think it was the largest fund of its kind at the time. We focused on turning around companies that had taken on excessive debt in the 1980s. We contributed our own capital in order to align our interests with those of our investors, and we didn't charge fees on each acquisition like many leveraged-buyout firms did. Instead, we used the funds to share risk with our investors—and to share opportunities. We had a stated objective of holding our investments for ten to twelve years. By 1995, we had invested almost all of the fund, which was a real accomplishment at a time when deal flow was almost at a standstill. Zell/Chilmark ended up owning Quality Food Centers, Carter Hawley Hale, Sealy Corporation, Schwinn Bicycle Company, and a number of other companies.

One of the fund's earliest investments was in Revco Discount Drug Stores. We agreed to provide the capital for the company as it was coming out of bankruptcy. There was a one- to two-month time frame between when the court awarded us the investment position and the transaction closed, and during that time, the interim CEO came to see me in Chicago. He made it very clear that he perceived me as just another board director—not as someone who would own 40 percent of the company. He was willing to send me periodic updates and that was about it. I explained that he would need to rethink this position for us to have a mutually productive relationship.

A few weeks later, this CEO sent the full board a whole new list of bylaws and provisions, all of which were designed to basically neuter the board's power and shift control of the company to the CEO. Included was a new executive compensation package that bordered on the preposterous. In it I noticed a provision that full vesting in the company's benefit program was granted to anyone over fifty-five. The CEO was fifty-seven. Needless to say, the board unanimously elected to change the CEO's position. This was in 1994, about six years after my epiphany with the

Santa Fe board, and it reinforced the importance of having owners, not just managers, provide leadership in an asset. Boards that don't exercise an ownership approach are complicit in poor-performing companies.

Probably the most memorable Zell/Chilmark deal for me was Jacor, a well-run, Cincinnati-based radio station owner with a bad balance sheet. From 1992 to 1996, we invested roughly $79 million for a 90 percent stake in Jacor. The company was overleveraged and on the verge of bankruptcy. We negotiated a complex restructuring with the company's senior lenders, subordinated lenders, and preferred equity holders to deleverage and restructure the company.

At that time, the FCC rule was that no company could own more than twenty radio stations per AM/FM band (or forty stations total) nationwide. So the radio business was all about shuffling stations, like playing cards, within that limit to get the best twenty stations you could find.

Shortly before we closed the deal, Randy Michaels and Terry Jacobs, who were running Jacor, came to me to finance the acquisition of a Denver station. Jacor already owned one of the other FM stations in Denver, and this one was losing money and available cheap. They showed up in Chicago carrying a thick book of details, prepared to make their pitch.

"This is a great deal," Randy assured me. He thumped the book on the table, ready to take me through it.

"Wait a minute," I said. "Do you understand the scope of the deal—why we should buy it?"

"Yes," he replied. "All the details are right here in this book." He added that he and Terry had worked feverishly night and day to prepare it.

I picked up the book and tossed it into a corner of my

office, where it landed with a thud. Randy and Terry stared at me wide-eyed.

"If you really understand it, you don't need a book," I said. "You could put it on a single piece of paper." They looked uncertain.

"I assume this says things are going to be great, right?" They nodded.

"What happens if you're wrong? How do I get out of the room?"

"What do you mean?" Randy asked.

"How bad can it get?"

"Well," he said, "it's pretty bad now, and if we fail to fix it you could lose some operating capital. But I don't see a station in Denver ever being worth less than $4 million. I mean, the building, the transmitter—the physical assets alone are worth close to that."

"Okay, great. How *good* could it get?"

The answer, in short, was *very* good. So I said, "Go do it."

And we got to work, always within the twenty-station limit. Our strategy was basically a hub-and-spoke approach to growth. We worked to reorganize the portfolio into a cluster of stations in high-growth areas, such as Denver or Tampa, and then bought other stations in the same region—allowing them to share management and programming and shore up their regional advertising bases.

Then, in February 1996, Congress passed the Telecommunications Act. Buried in that tome was a clause that eliminated the twenty-station-per-band cap and replaced it with a 50 percent market-share ceiling. In other words, companies could buy as many stations as they wanted as long as they didn't own more than 50 percent in any given market.

I read the act and immediately called up Randy. "Get on a plane to Chicago fast," I told him. When he arrived, I sat him down, and said, "Randy, this is one of the biggest moments in your career. I want you to go out and buy every radio station you can get your hands on in America. You buy them and I'll figure out how to finance them."

Timing and execution made all the difference. We earned most of our money on the first one hundred stations we bought—numbers 20 to 118. Why? Because after that the rest of the industry caught on, competition for stations increased, and prices went up. However, we continued to acquire even then, albeit at a slower rate, because of the economies of eliminating redundancies within a large portfolio in geographic concentrations and because our average price per station remained so low. But it was the first-mover advantage that made Jacor a lead dog—and a home run. Within three years, we went from 20 stations to 243.

Jacor was probably an asset I would have held for decades, but it was an investment through one of our private equity funds where we had promised investors a return of capital at the end of a predetermined period. So in late 1997, we started putting out feelers to sell the company. We had built an enviable portfolio and had syndicated some of the hottest radio personalities, including Rush Limbaugh, Dr. Laura Schlessinger, Leeza Gibbons, and Michael Reagan. Pretty much every broadcasting company expressed interest, including CBS and Clear Channel.

Clear Channel was a good fit to acquire Jacor for several reasons. I liked L. Lowry Mays, the founder and CEO. He promised to maintain Jacor's management, and from a portfolio standpoint there would be few issues for government regulators to raise.

So, in 1999, we sold Jacor to Clear Channel at the top of the industry cycle for $4.4 billion in stock and a total return of 1,237 percent. *That* was a fun investment.

The Jacor story was all about seeing micro opportunities in macro events. In this case, the macro event was legislation similar to the impact of the Economic Recovery Tax Act of 1981 on NOLs. But I find implications for opportunity everywhere—in world events, economic news, and conversations. I've always been on the lookout for big-picture influencers and anomalies that will direct the course of industries and companies.

But first-mover advantage requires conviction. While the rest of the radio industry was deliberating about what the telecom bill meant and how it would be implemented and whether it was a good change or a bad change, we *moved* and bought up every station we could find.

In total, the Zell/Chilmark fund made investments in ten companies in the grocery, radio, bedding, sports equipment, drugstore, and airline business sectors, and generated a 23.5 percent internal rate of return at 2.9 times invested capital from 1990 to 2000. After the fund's last investment in 1998, people called and asked me, "What's the next fund?" I said, "There is no next fund." The market had turned; the window for finding distressed assets at high discounts to replacement cost had passed. I didn't want to just be in the business of raising money. If I asked someone to give me money to invest, I had to have a specific thesis. I wasn't out to gobble up as much money as I could. Instead, I shifted to identifying investment opportunities for my own capital and for those I invited to join me.

• • •

We ended up leading seven IPOs totaling about $2 billion that decade—in manufacturing, travel, hardware, and real estate. We raised $1 billion for the Zell/Chilmark Fund and $2 billion for the Zell/Merrill real estate funds, and that was just equity. We also found another significant NOL deal (much like Itel and GAMI) with Danielson Holding Corporation in 1999. We ended up focusing Danielson around one investment, Covanta, and changing the company's name. Covanta is a global energy-from-waste company I still chair today. And I formed Equity International, the private investment firm that would focus on real estate in emerging markets. There was a lot going on and the scale of opportunity took our business to a whole new level.

On a personal front, as I've said, the early 1990s were rough. My second divorce in 1994 didn't help. Sharon and I had drifted apart. Technically, our separation had begun in 1983. She was spending a lot of time in Sun Valley, Idaho, and had built a life there, while my life was in Chicago. Over the years, I had just resolved that someone who had the responsibilities I had and whose goals required such an enormous amount of attention simply had to make a trade. There hadn't been a sense of urgency on either of our parts to make the break official. We were, after all—and still are—friends. By the time we did divorce, my life perspectives were starting to change, but more on that later.

CHAPTER SIX

Cassandra

One of my favorite quotes, paraphrased, is "Those who cannot remember the past are condemned to repeat it" by George Santayana. And no quote was more fitting for the real estate industry in the 1980s. A lot of so-called real estate professionals—many of whom had been through the bust just a decade earlier—didn't know what the hell they were doing. Once again, too many people got swept up in the fever of easy money and the perceived notion that we could build our cities to the sky.

The Black Monday stock market crash in October 1987 kicked off a new recession. In effect, we'd been borrowing on the future, and now the bill had come due. Since real estate tends to lag the general economy, the full impact to our industry was still years away, but by the end of 1987, I knew it was too late. I also knew that this time it was more than simply cyclical. We were looking at a seismic collapse, with lasting fundamental changes to the industry. I told people it was coming, but no one would listen. Unfortunately, when people live in a balloon, they tend to shy away from the guy holding the needle.

So I wrote an article titled "From Cassandra, With Love"

and it ran in the March 1988 *Real Estate Issues*. Cassandra was a character in Greek legend cursed by Apollo with the ability to make accurate predictions that no one believed. In my article, I presented a dire warning to the real estate industry, which, not surprisingly, no one took seriously.

I cited the panic I was seeing. It was fragmented but spreading. The downturn was being grossly underestimated. People were asking when it would end, but that was the wrong question.

This time, as I pointed out in my article, there was a *structural* change in real estate that went deeper than the normal peaks and valleys of a boom-bust cycle. Although oversupply was definitely a factor, the damage was compounded by other emerging realities in the marketplace.

I likened the fuzzy thinking to that of a postoperative patient waking up in the recovery room. Before he even knows the extent of the damage and the fix, his first reaction is that he's been through the worst of it and all will be well. But the prognosis of a patient suffering from a broken leg is radically different from one who just had his leg amputated. The newly awakened patient can't know the difference until the drugs wear off and the full reality of his situation sets in. In the real estate scenario, the drug was easy Japanese money, which led to overbuilding and overinvesting and simultaneously disguised massive permanent changes for the industry.

They included the obliteration of dedicated real estate lenders through the savings and loan crisis and extreme tax reform. S&Ls provided federally insured loans at long-term fixed interest rates. When inflation rose and the Fed doubled rates, S&Ls were no longer competitive for depositors and lost much of their business to money markets, depleting the banks' coffers. Out of desperation, many S&Ls made risky speculative loans and in some cases committed fraud, which exacerbated the scenario.

With S&Ls on life support, the Tax Reform Act of 1986 (TRA 86) dealt another crushing blow to the real estate industry by destroying one of the primary motivators of real estate investment— capital gains and other tax benefits. Until TRA 86, real estate investors were largely passive. Syndicates of investors (many of whom were doctors, lawyers, or businessmen like my father) pooled their money to buy properties and hired management companies to run them. They used the depreciation of real estate as a tax break to offset their other income. It was a sweet deal. But TRA 86 dramatically reduced the value of real estate as an investment to them by sharply limiting the tax benefits.

As I laid it out in my "Cassandra" article: "The prognostication herein represents a bitter pill to a consumptive and macho industry. Failure to recognize and differentiate between past overbuilding and structural change in demand, use and affordability will be viewed with the same historical reference held by those who opened the gates to Troy."

I got a lot of flak for that article. Some people said, "Sam keeps writing these pessimistic articles because he's trying to save all of the good deals for himself." What they didn't appreciate was that I wasn't *pessimistic*. I was *realistic*. Eyes wide open.

There was another big difference between the pending opportunities in the 1980s compared to the 1970s. In the 1970s, the real estate crisis created opportunities to buy assets at very cheap prices. Sellers provided financing because they didn't have to mark the assets down to market. In the 1980s, owners were going to have to take the write-downs. Therefore, to buy discounted assets, I would need a lot of cash.

So I called Merrill Lynch and said, "I want to create an opportunity fund wherein investors put up cash to become my partners in the purchase of distressed real estate." No one, including me, had done this kind of fund before, but they thought it was a great idea. They put up 5 percent of the first fund's target and said they'd raise the balance of the capital.

Six months later, we still had no commitments. Not one. So I took over the process and hit the road—from May 10 through June 30, 1989. I found that to raise money, I had to do it personally. I traveled with Merrill forty-two of those fifty-two days and did every single presentation—typically three to four a day in different cities. Now, those who know me know I am not a fan of wearing suits and ties. So I developed a ritual. As the plane was landing, I'd put on my suit and tie, go to the meeting, make the presentation, get back on the plane, and change back into jeans and a sweater. We'd head to the next city, and on landing, I'd get back into the monkey suit. And so on. I raised $400 million (about $785 million today), and at the closing dinner, the Merrill team gave me a pinstripe suit with a shirt and tie sewn in, and a zipper, so I could just step in and pull it up. For years afterward I had that suit on a stand in my office.

Anyway, when I started the road show, I quickly learned that the challenge in raising capital for our fund was that the guys we were pitching to didn't see the crisis; they were still at the party. So how could they see the opportunity?

Imagine the scene: I'd walk in the door and announce: "We're about to have the worst real estate debacle in history," and the guy would look at me and say, "What do you mean? We're at 12 percent this year in real estate." I had to get him to come to grips with what was really going on before I could even start to talk about the opportunity. I had to show him the vacancy rates and related metrics and prove to him that all the conditions were aligned for an epic fall. And then I had to assure him that we were going to make money, lots of it, by picking up the pieces.

Sure enough, over the next few years—into the early 1990s—the devastation became increasingly apparent. Most private real estate was leveraged at 80 to 90 percent and with falling occupancies and rents. Debt service became unsustainable. Many of the big real estate players that had dominated the industry for decades lost their shirts. It was called the worst real estate crisis since the Great Depression.

I coined the phrase "Stay Alive 'til '95" during an October 1990 industry event keynote address, and it became the industry mantra. My point was that when it was all said and done, it didn't matter how smart you were if you didn't have staying power, if you weren't able to hang on to your assets. Four years later, the market started showing signs of life; we were through the worst of it. So I commemorated our industry's struggle by rewriting the lyrics to "Stayin' Alive" by the Bee Gees and having the song recorded by professional singers. I commissioned a custom-designed iron sculpture/music box that depicted four executives trying desperately to prop up a tilting office building. I sent a few hundred of them to leaders in the real estate industry.

As an aside, the annual gifts I had been creating since the 1970s had grown increasingly elaborate (the downside to a personality with a need to test limits). Today they are in the form of customized automata—moving mechanical music box sculptures. The recipient list has grown as well, to include a group of about six hundred friends, colleagues, and business associates. I get a kick out of the reactions each year when the gifts are delivered. You can see them lined up on the shelves in select executives' offices in this and other countries. Recipients play them for friends and talk about the lyrics. They are at least a novelty and at best a conversation starter that defines our Equity brand as singular.

Here are my revised lyrics to the Bee Gees' hit "Stayin' Alive."

Well you can tell by the way I've walked my talk
I'm a real estate man, it's time to talk:
Market's been cold but it's getting warm
We've been kicked around since Tax Act Reform
But now it's all right, it's OK
We've lived to see another day
We set out to understand replacement cost and where it stands
Whether you're a banker or whether you're an owner
You're stayin' alive, 'til '95
Feel the winds a-blowin', occupancy's growing'
And we're stayin' alive, 'til '95
Ah, ha, ha, ha, stayin' alive.

When the retrospective analysis was done years later, estimates of the total losses in the real estate industry for this period exceeded $80 billion, and commercial property values had fallen by up to 50 percent.

The Zell/Merrill funds were perfectly positioned to cherry-pick the assets being littered around the country. But as hard as it had been to raise the money, at first it was just as hard to invest it. We were so early that sellers had no idea what properties were worth, so they kept postponing their decisions. Finally, markets and values began to stabilize, and lenders became anxious to get real estate off of their books. I was the only buyer out there.

By 1995, we had assembled an impressive collection of trophy office buildings and were starting to think about taking the portfolio public in a REIT. So when Rockefeller Center in Manhattan came into play, I pursued it, thinking the asset would be the proverbial icing on our office-portfolio cake in a public offering.

It was a serious battle for a serious asset. I used to joke that I wished I'd owned the movie rights to the deal. It had big players—the Japanese real estate giant Mitsubishi, David Rockefeller, the Agnelli family, Goldman Sachs, General Electric, and Walt Disney. An unbelievable cast.

At the peak of Japanese investment in real estate in the 1980s, Mitsubishi had purchased an 80 percent interest in Rockefeller Group Inc., the partnership entity that owned Rock Center. Behind this transaction was a $1.3 billion mortgage held by a newly formed REIT, RCPI. In May 1995, when ownership was unable to service its debt in a weakening market, it went into default on the mortgage, thus cutting off RCPI's primary source of revenue, and the REIT filed for bankruptcy. We proposed a deal to infuse $250 million into the asset for a 50 percent interest in RCPI with the goal of eventually taking full ownership.

This was probably the last deal where I was front and center on every aspect of the negotiations. The intensity of the transaction was like none I had ever experienced—relentless conference calls and unending one-on-one meetings. I also received a lot of unwanted publicity, including the assumption that my motivations were more about ego than economics. But nothing could have been further from the truth, as anyone who knows me understands. In the end, we were unable to bridge the abyss, and Rock Center went to a joint venture comprising Goldman Sachs, Tishman Speyer, and David Rockefeller.

While there were many impediments in our negotiations, there was little doubt throughout the process that there was no enthusiasm for a Chicago guy to buy an icon of New York City at a discount. I think there are certain assets that are particularly vulnerable to being "hometowned," and Rock Center was one of them.

In all, we raised four Zell/Merrill funds from 1989 through 1996 for an aggregate total of $2.1 billion. Although we bought different asset classes, our primary target was high-quality office buildings, which we bought at significant discounts to replacement cost.

Incidentally, when the market crashed again twenty years later, in 2008, my phone rang off the hook with people eager to join me on a grave-dancing buying binge. For the next few years, I had to repeatedly explain that this was a whole different recession. I would not be raising a fund because there was no wave of grave-dancing opportunities in commercial real estate. With low to nonexistent interest rates, there was no cost to lenders to carry assets on their books. Now the real estate lending industry's mantra was "Extend and pretend." A rolling loan carries no loss. In other words, leveraged property owners could extend maturing loans until conditions improved. Since they weren't forced to sell, there was no flood of bargains.

By the early 1990s, real estate owners were desperate for capital, and there was only one place left to turn: the capital markets. Richard Saltzman of Merrill Lynch was a strong steward of the modern REIT era with financing innovations and insights into the potential for the industry.

I took my first real estate company public in 1993. In addition to the Zell/Merrill funds, we had spent the previous two decades amassing an enormous portfolio in other asset classes. We debuted our real estate holdings on the New York Stock Exchange with Manufactured Home Communities (MHC), now known as Equity LifeStyle Properties (ELS), and its forty-seven manufactured home communities. It was one of the early companies to list as a REIT in the modern commercial real estate era.

Today, ELS is the largest owner of manufactured home communities and recreational vehicle (RV) parks in the country, and continues to be one of my favorite companies. ELS has produced one of the most consistently high returns (17 percent average annually) of any REIT since its IPO. And it was a contrarian play.

The image of manufactured homes is down-market. People think of a transient, low-class setting, with a guy in a ripped T-shirt drinking beer and grilling hot dogs outside a rundown box and yelling "Stella!" like Marlon Brando in *A Streetcar Named Desire*. That was my perception, anyway.

But then in 1984, during the due diligence on a deal, we were analyzing the competition and we discovered MHC.

We were one of the largest owners of real estate in the country, but we knew nothing about manufactured housing parks. So I sent one of my senior investment guys to Florida to check it out. He called me practically babbling, "I don't believe what I'm seeing," he said. "I've been looking at these mobile homes . . ."

"Not good?" I asked.

"No, no, you don't understand," he cried. "These are fabulous assets. They're phenomenal!"

And they were. The MHC portfolio, which was owned by Trizec Properties, was one of the largest premier portfolios of this asset class in the country. The sites were beautiful—lakeside, oceanfront, wooded, landscaped. I couldn't believe it. They were like stylish subdivisions. They had porches and garages and clubhouses and golf courses.

So we looked at the numbers and found that there was also a strong risk-to-reward ratio. There was constrained supply due to NIMBY (not in my backyard) regulations that created barriers to entry, making the development of new communities very difficult. And the portfolio had about a 1 percent turnover rate. Once residents moved to the parks, they seldom left.

Believe me when I say that when we bought into manufactured homes, *nobody* in the sophisticated real estate world had ever gone close to one of these communities. It wasn't even on their radar screens. But we didn't care that we were going to get labeled as mobile home guys or hear jokes about being "trailer trash." We were nomads in search of opportunities and returns.

Taking a company in the manufactured home business public was no easy shot. It took all my creativity and skills to explain to the guys on the Street why this business was a winner. So we created T-shirts to drive the message home. The cartoon graphic was me strangling a guy above a caption that read "For the last time, pencil neck, it's not called a trailer!" Eventually, the IPO was very successful, although not everyone was persuaded. I remember one investor who was particularly skeptical. When *Barron's* wrote an article before the IPO, it quoted him essentially saying that he wouldn't lower himself to a mobile home venture. "I'm going to take a pass," he said. So when we completed the IPO and it was oversubscribed five to one, I sent the guy a football with a note saying "If you're going to pass, maybe this will help."

About twelve years into ELS's life as a public company, its growth stalled. Business was great, but there was little to no supply in the industry to acquire. Manufactured home site owners realized these were great long-term assets, and they weren't selling. And the same NIMBY phenomenon that had made this sector so appealing also prevented us from developing.

We set about solving the problem and discovered that RV parks had the same fundamental characteristics as manufactured home communities. They were smaller versions of the same business model—we'd own the land while tenants would own the structures, and there was low turnover. The sectors also had similar tenant demographics, the same types of sites, and the same cash flow characteristics.

So, ELS became the first company to combine and institutionalize the blended asset classes. Ironically, the manufactured home industry was almost as parochial about expanding its definition to include RV sites as the real estate industry had been to include manufactured home sites.

Today ELS has a huge portfolio of manufactured home and RV "resorts"—the best in the United States. It controls over 140,000 sites in thirty-two states and British Columbia. Since its 1993 IPO, ELS's market cap of $296 million has grown to over $6 billion.

Later that year, we also took Equity Residential (EQR), our 17,000-unit apartment building portfolio, public. The evolution of EQR is one of the best representations of the seismic demographic shift occurring in the U.S. At its IPO twenty-five years ago, EQR comprised primarily suburban garden apartments, the gold standard for multifamily at the time. The most coveted assets had expressway frontage visibility, which was a primary marketing tool before the Internet revolutionized the way people found apartments. I remember banners on our buildings along the freeway that read: "If you lived here you'd be home by now."

By the early 2000s, I saw on the horizon what I believed would be the single largest cultural change of my lifetime—the deferral of marriage. Unlike me and my college friends, who were all married the first year out of college, people were waiting longer and longer to tie the knot. Each generation has had at least a 10 percent decline in marriage by age thirty-two. I knew singles would want to stay close to the action and that they'd sacrifice almost anything, specifically square footage, to do it, and they'd also pay more. They would want less living space and more community space. So we set out to reshape EQR's portfolio from garden apartments in suburbia to high-rises in 24/7 cities. We completed that transformation in 2015. EQR ended that year with a market cap of $30 billion and an irreplaceable assemblage of apartment buildings in the country's best six barrier-to-entry markets.

Today, instead of expressway frontage, apartments are measured by their "walk scores"—how many steps to public transportation, to the grocery store, to Starbucks, to the gym. Go deeper and you can see the changes from the deferral of marriage across industries. The shift in priorities, lifestyle, and discretionary income that began in the 1990s was a harbinger for a new era of consumerism. Real estate isn't just about buildings as inanimate objects. It often reflects the pulse of the nation.

I like to say I didn't invent the modern REIT industry, but I helped make it dance. My role was focused on strong corporate governance. My goal was to secure the industry as an independent asset class with its own allocation among institutional investors. It took a lot of lobbying and preaching in front of my peers, pension funds, insurance companies, banks, and politicians. The idea that real estate could graduate into the upper class of corporate America was absurd at the time. But by force of will I knew we could get there.

In late 1992, while working on the Taubman Centers IPO, Morgan Stanley created the UPREIT structure. It was actually just another version of existing corporate reorganization provisions, but it had never been applied to the real estate industry.

It was a game changer. The UPREIT provided property

owners with a way to contribute assets to an entity in exchange for operating units, which could be converted, one for one, to REIT shares, and thereby defer the tax consequences. In other words, the UPREIT established a methodology for large holders of real estate to create liquidity without triggering a taxable event, as long as the holders didn't sell their shares. The structure allowed the majority of major private real estate holders to incorporate their portfolios into the public sector.

Many of us—the new leaders of the real estate industry—immediately saw the potential in this new vehicle, but there are always people who prefer the status quo. At a 1994 National Association of Real Estate Investment Trusts (NAREIT) annual event in the Netherlands, one member of the executive committee got up and challenged the validity of the structure and its benefits to the industry. I was outraged and later called the head of NAREIT. I gave him an option: Either get rid of the executive, or I would start my own UPREIT association. The good news is that my subtlety worked.

Indeed, the UPREIT has been all it promised to be. As the REIT industry has stretched into other countries, foreign legislation has not allowed for the UPREIT structure; the embedded tax liability has precluded the benefits of taking private portfolios public, and that has dramatically impeded growth—and opportunity for investors.

Step back in time and you'll see that the birth of the public REIT industry was an enormous transformation from the "dark ages," when commercial real estate was shrouded in mystery. Nobody but insiders could figure it out. Brokers held all the cards, and they weren't telling. There was no visibility into markets or assets, and there were no metrics. The opaque nature of the industry contributed to overbuilding and cycle extremes.

Further, real estate operators had a reputation for ignoring the best interests of the shareholders and often used early REITs as a dumping ground for lower-quality assets.

By the time of the first modern REIT in 1993, I had the advantage of having spent the last decade schooling myself in the public markets for our corporate companies. I was very familiar with what worked on Wall Street and what was expected of great companies. And I knew the real estate industry was starting with a reputational deficit.

In 1993, I was appointed to the executive committee of NAREIT, and I gave a speech at the annual meeting. I said our latest entry into the public markets reminded me of a bumper sticker I once saw in Houston, Texas, in 1984. It said: PLEASE GOD, GIVE US ONE MORE OIL BOOM AND WE PROMISE WE WON'T SCREW IT UP.

I went on to outline what our industry had to do if it was going to thrive on Wall Street. Boiled down, it was all about transparency, predictability, and accountability. We had to earn investors' trust. That meant creating REITs with high-quality properties, maintaining low debt to equity ratios, selling present income rather than future expectations, and ensuring sponsors and managers had skin in the game and were incentivized to grow shareholder value.

The REIT mafia, a small collection of investment funds that had the weight to heavily influence the direction of the industry, embraced this transformation, and we ended up growing the industry from $7 billion in the early 1990s to over $1 trillion in 2016. Today, they are a respected asset class that has earned inclusion on the S&P 500.

The simple genius of public REITs is that they turn bricks and mortar into transparent and predictable liquid assets. And because they are required to distribute at least 90 percent of their taxable income to shareholders each year, they tend to provide high dividends. By virtue of their lower leverage, the commercial real estate industry as a whole is much less cyclical and volatile. Just look at the way it weathered the Great Recession of 2008, in contrast to single-family real estate. I couldn't be more proud of the industry I grew up in and that gave me so much, and I consider my role in this evolution one of the biggest accomplishments of my career.

In the late 1990s, about ten years after I wrote the "Cassandra" article, the dot-com bubble was inflating. The market was in a frenzy over every new website.

Being first with an idea was enough. Getting more "eyeballs" on your site was enough. Giving away grocery delivery, or pet food delivery, or online quizzes was enough. But I couldn't see where the revenues were going to come from.

I remember sitting at dinner on New Year's Eve in 1999, mere months before everything went south. I was vacationing in the south of France with a group of friends, all of whom were sophisticated businesspeople. I looked around the table and asked them a simple question: "Yahoo's market cap today is $100 billion. If I gave you $25 billion in cash, is there any one of you who doesn't think you could reproduce what Yahoo has done to date?" The conversation validated that market valuations had completely disconnected from reality.

Although a few people put up a pretty good fight, ultimately everyone acknowledged that they could probably do it. Which meant there were no barriers to entry. And of course there was still that pesky little problem of revenues.

By then my creative team had already completed the annual gift I had started six months earlier. It was, of course, a music sculpture depicting "The Emperor Has No Clothes." I wrote the lyrics, an irreverent—and, it turns out, prescient—takedown of the inflated valuations of tech companies at the time. The musical message was to the tune of "50 Ways to Leave Your Lover":

The problem is all inside your head she said to me
The answer is easy if you think less logically
I'd like to help you all get rich at 23
There must be 50 ways to make a billion . . .
Just add a dot com, Tom
Front your name with an E, Lee
Start auctioning toys, Roy
And set yourself free . . .
But she never said what happens in cold economic light
Are the emperor's clothes on,
will discount cash flows dictate flight?
So I wonder, can all this cyber math be right?
Are there 50 ways to make a billion?

Like Cassandra, it seemed I was destined to be disbelieved when my hypotheses went against conventional wisdom. The trick, of course, is in monetizing those hypotheses. By 1997, our business wasn't just cash flow positive again. It was exploding. The IPOs had generated liquidity; we had raised $1 billion for the Zell/Chilmark fund and over $2 billion for the Zell/Merrill fund. We had survived, and I had sustained the business Bob and I had built together.

It was that year that I decided to turn the Zell/Merrill office building portfolio into a REIT. By then, we had four funds with many investors, active and passive—pension funds, insurance companies, and individuals. They had originally invested in Zell/Merrill under one set of assurances, understandings, and format. Now we were asking them to embrace a whole new opportunity, accepting "unproven" REIT stock in return for their interests. Talk about herding cats. Naturally they had questions about what the stock would be worth, trading volume, quarterly dividends, and a slew of other issues. And we couldn't answer a lot of them. But they leaped, and in 1997, we went public with Equity Office Properties (EOP) Trust.

We debuted on the New York Stock Exchange with ninety buildings comprising more than 32 million square feet of office space across the country. We had institutional-quality tenants with an average lease term of seven years, which provided us with visibility into a predictable stream of revenue. And we offered a 5.7 percent dividend. I had no doubt we could grow the platform and that Equity Office would be a hit on Wall Street. And it was, at least for a while.

CHAPTER SEVEN

A Godfather Offer

Timing is everything. That's just a trite phrase until you actually find yourself in a situation when you've closed the biggest transaction in history on the cusp of a catastrophic collapse in the global real estate market. But perfect timing is revealed only in hindsight. So when I completed the $39 billion sale of Equity Office in early 2007, I didn't yet know how the story would play out.

I believed real estate values at the time were about as high as they were going to go. All signs were pointing to the end of the cycle. But that's not why I did the deal.

Equity Office was the largest REIT in the country. We had spent a decade acquiring an irreplaceable collection of over five hundred of the best office buildings in every major market in the U.S. It was my baby. Truth is, had I kept the company private, I probably would have never considered selling. But when I took EOP public, I assumed a fiduciary responsibility to shareholders. In exchange for their capital, I made a commitment to give them the best return possible on their investment. That was my primary obligation. Nothing stood before that. And I backed that commitment with my own money as the largest private shareholder. Not that I expected a sale to happen. I thought Equity Office was too big to be acquired.

When we launched the IPO for Equity Office, a central hypothesis of our strategy was "bigger is better." We thought we could achieve economies of scale to drive down costs, which would improve our rates of return. In cities where we owned a large number of buildings, we wouldn't need separate management staffs. We could reduce redundancies; buy services and materials, such as cleaning and light bulbs, in bulk; and collectively market the assets. Turned out, that was all true, but we could increase margins only so much.

Equity Office was born out of EGI's entrepreneurial culture. The management team came straight from one of my private companies, where we encouraged creativity and smart risk taking and made allowances for ideas that didn't work. We tested innovative strategies, such as advertising in and on our buildings—commonplace now but leading edge in the early 2000s. We set up unusual retail leasing strategies. We also tried to capitalize on our size and scale by negotiating omnibus leases with giant tenants like IBM and Bank of America. Since major corporations leased in many cities and at multiple locations, we hoped to sign them to national lease agreements. This would provide us with certainty of revenue and a competitive advantage while giving them maximum flexibility to grow or shrink throughout their portfolios. As part of this effort, every year we hosted an elaborate event for the national leasing guys of the country's largest companies. I remember being at one of the dinners in San Francisco and talking to a guy from a multinational company. He went on and on about how great Equity Office was, how easy we made his life, how efficient we were, and so on. And then the following year, he signed a lease at a competing building across the street for $1 less per square foot.

So not everything we tried worked. But underlying it all was Class A office product—and we were the largest owner in all but a couple of the country's top markets. Further, some of our cities, like Boston and San Francisco, had high barriers to new supply.

I knew what the Equity Office portfolio was worth. And I knew we were undervalued by Wall Street. Every quarter, the management team would do an in-depth analysis of every asset in the portfolio to develop a real-time valuation. The most reliable measure of our buildings' value remained—and had always been, in my opinion—replacement cost. Replacement cost mattered more to me than rents or comparable prices or vacancies or economic growth or stock price. This was because replacement cost determined the price of future competition.

We had done a merger in 2000 that negatively influenced market perception until the day we sold Equity Office seven years later. It involved Spieker Properties, our single biggest acquisition at $7.3 billion. Spieker was a West Coast REIT, based in Menlo Park, California, that owned 40 million square feet, mostly of office space, throughout Silicon Valley.

Ned Spieker, the company's chairman, called me late in 2000 to say he had been approached about selling his company, though he hadn't decided whether to do so. Clearly, he was looking for a better price.

At that point, the dot-com meltdown had already begun in earnest, and the NASDAQ composite of high-tech companies was down nearly 40 percent from its peak the previous March. I'd seen it coming and been vocal about it. I wasn't surprised that many Internet companies in the San Francisco–San Jose corridor were retrenching or walking away from their office leases. So the marketplace was baffled by our move to acquire Spieker at what looked like the top of the tech industry market. Needless to say, a long-term strategy doesn't always sync with Wall Street's quarter-to-quarter view. But we were in real estate, not tech, and I had a big-picture plan. The deal was an opportunity to dominate an office market that was home to Apple, Google, and most of the other leading tech companies in the world. If we passed, it was likely the portfolio might sell, either in whole or in pieces, to another player.

It was frustrating that we couldn't get the Street to see past the timing of the Spieker merger and recognize the underlying value we had created. But I was confident that it was only a matter of time.

So we ignored the noise and kept going, turning our focus to further sculpting our holdings. As with EQR, we used changing demographics as our guide. The suburban corporate campuses built in the 1970s and 1980s to accommodate a short commute by CEOs were dinosaurs. To access young talent, companies had to centralize in 24/7 cities. We did the same, and by 2006 we had culled our portfolio to include almost exclusively Class A office space in every major central business district in the country. The predictable cash flow from high-quality assets also reflected a premise we had applied in the past. This mix of assets and markets would achieve the highest rent growth in good economies and had the least risk of vacancies in down economies.

The first bid for Equity Office, when it came, barely registered on my radar.

It was from an unlikely suitor. One day in November 2005, Richard Kincaid, Equity Office's chief executive officer, received an exploratory offer of $25 billion from an investment adviser for the California Public Employees' Retirement System (CALPERS).

A Godfather Offer

The CALPERS advisers told Richard they thought Equity Office was grossly undervalued by the market and worth $34 or $35 a share, particularly in light of the rapidly rising prices being paid for office buildings. All true, except at that point, I thought we were worth at least $40 a share. It was a nice try, but I wasn't interested.

A few months later, in January 2006, CALPERS came knocking again, this time represented by a team of advisers from Lehman Brothers. We opened our books to them, but I still thought the price they were talking about, which ranged from the mid-$30s to $40 per share, was too low for us to consider.

Over the summer, Steve Roth, chairman of Vornado Realty, approached me. Steve told me he was interested in a merger involving the exchange of stock. We kept talking to Vornado through October, though a stock merger didn't look attractive. Coincidentally, at that point our stock price began a sharp rise as the investment world got more interested in buying office buildings and the value of our assets became apparent. We were on the upswing, but I still wasn't selling.

Then, in mid-August, Blackstone Group called us informally with an offer of $40 to $42 a share. Blackstone had a partner; it was allied with Brookfield, another REIT, which would have acquired about a third of our portfolio. We told Blackstone the bid was insufficient. Still, we were a little bit surprised to have such a robust offer. Suddenly I realized that my too-big-to-sell company might sell after all.

In September, we heard from Blackstone again. This time, Brookfield was out of the picture. Richard sat down with Jon Gray, the thirty-six-year-old head of Blackstone's real estate division, for a preliminary discussion about selling some of our buildings. Gray was an up-and-comer who'd been with Blackstone since graduating from college. He was an impressive guy; I predicted great things for him early in his career, and I wasn't wrong. A decade later, he'd be a rainmaker at the top of the industry.

Serious and detail oriented, Gray didn't overlook even a stray remark. When Richard told him our board had decided against selling the company, Gray asked under what circumstances that decision might change. Recalling what I'd often told him, Richard said, "Sam says it has to be a Godfather offer—too good to refuse." Evidently the allusion to *The Godfather* stuck in Gray's mind. Toward the end of October, we got a call from our bankers at Merrill Lynch. They said that Gray had called wanting to know what a "Godfather offer" looked like.

It was the right question. I told Richard to let Blackstone know that Equity Office wasn't on the market, but a bid of over $45 a share could make things interesting.

In a bullish move, Blackstone came back with an offer of $47.50 a share. Now we had to listen. On November 12, we held a board meeting to discuss the offer. I was torn, because if it was my company alone, I could have rejected the offer. But Blackstone's offer was well north of what we knew was the value of our real estate.

I have always believed that every day you choose to hold an asset, you are also choosing to buy it. Would I buy our buildings at the price Blackstone was quoting? Nope.

In very short order, we were able to persuade Blackstone to raise its bid to $48.50 a share for a total of $20 billion, plus $16 billion in debt, or $36 billion total. I insisted that our agreement include an unusually small breakup fee so other potential bidders wouldn't be discouraged. The typical breakup fee is up to 3 percent of the selling price, but I set ours at $200 million— around 1 percent of the offer's equity value. Obviously, this didn't sit well with Blackstone, but it was not negotiable.

As an aside, the deal's terms also included a provision that precluded Blackstone from sharing any information about our transaction. As a result, they could not prearrange sales of any of the buildings to help offset the risk of their bet. This would turn out to be a critical negotiating point to secure the highest price possible for Equity Office later on.

The sale agreement with Blackstone was announced on November 19, 2006.

Now the real fun began. I viewed our agreement as a floor for an auction, and I was hoping to see other bidders enter the fray—in particular, CALPERS and Vornado.

There is a finite number of M&A bankers and real estate lenders of the caliber to work this level of transaction, and every one of them wanted in on either our or Blackstone's deal team. This was the biggest deal in real estate's history, and everyone wanted to be part of it.

It would have been easy for Blackstone to suck the air out of the room for other bidders by engaging all of the key players in some capacity. But I sought and received assurance from Gray that wouldn't be an issue.

This stance created a fair amount of grumbling among bankers. Merrill Lynch was handling the deal for us, and Bank of America for Blackstone, but others wanted a piece of the action. JPMorgan Chase called Richard and me, aggressively urging us to hire them for the deal, but I wanted to keep JPMorgan Chase available in case a competing bidder materialized.

Although our agreement with Blackstone precluded me from soliciting competing bids, I sure as hell wasn't going to discourage one if it was out there. And there was: Steve Roth and Vornado. Steve had been circling around the idea of a purchase for some time, but our earlier conversations hadn't yielded any doable numbers. I'd known Steve since the 1970s, and I liked and respected him—especially his long-term view for real estate. While Blackstone was most certainly planning to unload properties once they bought the company, Steve expressed an interest in waiting out the market and holding the assets. He believed in Equity Office as an assemblage. But it didn't really matter whether I liked Steve or his plan. I had to choose the best deal for my shareholders.

It wasn't clear whether Steve would even make a bid, but the rumors were generating a lot of interest in the market, and by January 2007, Equity Office's share price was above the Blackstone offer based on the talk of a Vornado bid. In mid-January I sent Steve an email:

> Dear Stevie:
>
> Roses are red
>
> Violets are blue
>
> I heard a rumor
>
> Is it true?
>
> Love and kisses,
>
> Sam

I later learned that my suggestive rhyme arrived as Steve was in Vornado's boardroom, huddling with bankers and lawyers. When his secretary handed him my email, he felt that he had to respond in kind:

> Sam, how are you?
>
> The rumor is true
>
> I do love you

A Godfather Offer

> And the price is $52.
>
> To see if this poem will rhyme
>
> We should talk at a set time
>
> While to talk like this is nifty
>
> We should really talk at three fifty.
>
> Forever yours,
>
> Steve

He was true to his word. Steve had put together a consortium composed of Vornado Realty, Starwood Capital, and Walton Street Capital—all heavy-duty real estate players with strong leadership and credentials. On January 17, they submitted a preliminary bid of $52 a share, with 40 percent in Vornado common stock and the remainder in cash. They had lined up financing from JPMorgan Chase, Lehman Brothers, UBS, Barclays Capital, and Royal Bank of Scotland. A few days later, we granted them access to our books, as we had to Blackstone, to gather facts for a formal bid.

The game was on.

If you do deals for a living, you know the energy that a big one generates. It's intoxicating; the air crackles with the energy of anticipation. You are bouncing on your toes all day, every day. It is, quite simply, really fun.

But with the Vornado deal, as with all deals, the devil was in the details, and I could see some holes in the offer.

Blackstone's ace in the hole was that it was offering an all-cash deal, as opposed to Vornado's 40 percent stock. Blackstone was also aggressive about a quick deal closing, promising to close the transaction within two weeks of a scheduled Equity Office shareholders meeting on February 5, while Vornado had to wait a few months for its own shareholders' vote and for the SEC's ruling because of the proposed issuance of Vornado stock. A lot can happen in a few months, and I liked the certainty Blackstone was offering.

Steve Schwarzman, Blackstone's chairman and CEO, was outspoken in the press about wanting to avoid a nasty bidding war, and to prove his point, he upped the offer to $54 a share in cash, or $38.3 billion including debt. We accepted Blackstone's revised offer and agreed to raise the breakup fee to $500 million from $200 million. Now it would cost Vornado or anyone else an additional $300 million, or about $0.75 per share, to trump Blackstone.

Steve Roth was pushing me to put a heavier focus on his offer. I just kept telling him, "Steve, Blackstone's offer is all cash. Your offer is roughly half stock, half cash. In order for you to deliver, you have to have a shareholders' meeting and you have to get it approved. You have to get through the SEC. That means, in my judgment, six months. You're offering 50 cents per share more but at the cost of a six-month risk. I can't do it." In such a volatile market six months was a lifetime.

But Steve wasn't ready to give up. On February 1, Vornado raised its bid to $56 a share, this time agreeing to increase the cash portion to $31, which now represented 55 percent of the price. The amount was higher than its earlier bid, but the proportion of cash was slightly lower.

Blackstone had a right, under the terms of the original agreement, to match any competing bid. We also issued a statement saying we continued to recommend the Blackstone bid to shareholders, because the transaction it was proposing would close more quickly and would be paid in cash.

Vornado came back on Sunday, February 4, with a nonbinding offer to carry out the merger in two steps, thus speeding up payment of the cash portion to three weeks from acceptance of the bid. Vornado's purpose was to allay concerns of the Equity Office board that the length of time to close the deal, plus the uncertainty of the stock portion, increased the risk.

The clock was ticking. As the countdown to Equity Office's Monday night shareholder meeting approached, it felt like everyone was holding their breath.

Unquestionably, Blackstone held the lead, though what could it hurt to find out if it might raise its bid further? Monday morning, Richard called Jon Gray to see if Blackstone was willing to increase its $54-a-share bid. Gray said he'd get back to us later in the day.

Late Monday afternoon, Gray returned Richard's call. Yes, Blackstone was willing to raise its bid to $55.25 a share if we would raise the breakup fee to $700 million from $500 million. We discussed the proposal and sent Richard back to Gray to see if he would raise the bid to $55.50. Gray returned the call shortly afterward to say $55.50 was fine—again, as long as the breakup fee was raised to $720 million and we removed the provision about information sharing so they could line up asset sales to close immediately after our sale. This was significant to Blackstone; it helped them mitigate their risk. We agreed, and Blackstone immediately began lining up deals at premium prices. (This would be the pivotal reason why Blackstone ended up doing very well from our deal together.)

After the market closed on Monday, the board met to compare

the two bids. Merrill Lynch's bankers estimated that in present value terms, Vornado's $56 bid actually was worth between $54.81 and $55.07 a share, considering the various risks involved. It was Merrill's opinion that Blackstone's bid was strong—$55.50 per share for a transaction value of $39 billion including the assumption of debt for our treasured 543-building portfolio. We voted as a board to accept it. Our lawyers from Sidley Austin LLP amended the agreement, and we issued an announcement the next morning, February 6, 2007, before the market opened.

It was done. Equity Office had entered the public arena with an IPO price of $21 a share in 1997. Ten years later, it was exiting at $55.50—after having collected $16.48 per share in dividends for its ten years in the public domain. The sale was the largest leveraged buyout—in any industry—at the time.

Afterward, I sent Franck Muller watches to Steve Roth, Vornado CEO Michael Fascitelli, and Starwood chairman Barry Sternlicht. The inscription read: "Timing is Everything."

Was it the result I wanted? Obviously, having competing bidders drove up the price, so it was a good deal for shareholders. People have often asked me if I had a horse in the race—if I preferred one over the other. More specifically, they wanted to know if I preferred Steve Roth by virtue of our long relationship. The answer is a definitive no. I never allow my personal feelings to interfere with my duty to the shareholders, or even with my own private investments. Sentimentality about an asset leads to a lack of discipline. Steve understood perfectly, although even years later he would say he regretted losing Equity Office. Frankly, if our positions had been reversed, he would have done the same thing. As for any attachment I felt for the company I had nurtured from infancy, I had moved on. Once the deal was done, it was over for me. I had no remorse. I didn't think about it anymore.

To this day, people credit me with calling the top of the market when I sold Equity Office. The reality is, I wasn't trying to. While I was certain the market was frothy, I wasn't selling to get out of the office market. I had simply received a Godfather offer.

CHAPTER EIGHT

Zero Visibility

Risk is the ultimate differentiator. I have always had a deep and complex relationship with it. I am not a reckless person, but taking risks is really the only way to consistently achieve above-average returns—in life as well as in investments. My father proved that when he left Poland.

I am probably more comfortable with risk than most people. That's because I do as much as I can to understand it. To me, risk-taking rests on the ability to see all the variables and then identify the ones that will make or break you.

Sure, I'm always looking for unlocked potential, for strong fundamentals in a business that suggest a high probability of success. But everybody wants to look at how good a deal can get. People love focusing on the upside. That's where the fun is. What amazes me is how superficially they consider the downside. For me, the calculation in making a deal *starts* with the downside. If I can identify that, then I understand the risk I'm taking. What's the outcome if everything goes wrong? What actions would we take? Can I bear the cost? Can I survive it?

One of my best examples of this was Carter Hawley Hale

(CHH), the department store chain we owned in the 1990s. CHH was Zell/Chilmark Fund's first acquisition. It had been a venerable company with over eighty stores and had spun off brands like Waldenbooks and Neiman Marcus. At its peak in 1984, CHH was the sixth-largest department store chain in the U.S., but in 1991 it filed for Chapter 11. By then, it had sold off most of its really profitable businesses, and its core regional stores in the West, mostly in California, were suffering from growing competition in the region.

While we were deciding whether to buy the company, I sent one of my guys, David Contis, to do the due diligence. My then wife, Sharon, had met David when he was a kid working as a produce manager at a local grocery store. She was impressed with his energy and drive and invited him to the house to meet me. David ended up working for me off and on for about thirty years and went on to a great career in real estate.

I told David, "Go look at every store and its entire inventory, who we would sell it to and what we would get for it, in case the deal goes south." It was a basic fire-sale analysis—what we'd get in the worst-case scenario if we had to liquidate the company. David came back and said, "We'd get 80 percent of our purchase price back." So I knew that what we had to lose was 20 percent.

We bought roughly $550 million of the company's bonds and trade claims for 47 cents on the dollar, or $220 million. When the company came out of bankruptcy, those claims would be converted into stock. After all was said and done, we controlled over 70 percent of the equity. We owned the company for three years, and it was just horrible. In a relatively narrow window of time, CHH's California stores were impacted by earthquakes, riots, and fires. It was like the ten plagues. Revenues plummeted.

In 1995, we sold the company to Federated Department Stores—for 80 percent of our original purchase price.

We lost just about $50 million—20 percent of our investment—but to this day I consider that investment a success. Our risk analysis was exactly right. We went into the deal knowing we could lose $50 million, and we were willing to risk it for the potential upside.

In addition to looking at worst-case scenarios, I look at how hard something is to execute. The simpler the goals and the steps to reach them, the more likely I'll be successful. And if they aren't simple to begin with, I look at how I can untangle the complexities.

But no matter how much time you put into addressing risk, sometimes there are unforeseen events that blindside you. We're good at fixing problems when we catch them early enough, but unexpected external events can leave you with no chance to respond. And they can be disastrous. Of course, none was worse in our lifetime than September 11, 2001. It was an indelible heartbreak. And in the months that followed, as the country struggled to regain its footing, the economy and, in particular, the travel industry, were devastated.

In 1993, we had invested in a bankrupt company called American Hawaii Cruises and merged it into our existing cruise ship company, American Classic Voyages. American Hawaii had a fleet of two ships built in the 1950s, was overleveraged, and had no solid business strategy. They operated interisland Hawaiian tours. Passengers would fly in and out of Hawaii and stay on American Hawaii's ships so they could travel between the islands at night and spend very few waking hours at sea.

The opportunity was in the fact that maritime law, in the

form of the Jones Act, prevents foreign-built or foreign-flagged ships from conducting coastal trade in the U.S. In the case of tourism, foreign vessels have to either drop off or pick up passengers from a non-U.S. port, certainly not convenient for interisland vacationing in Hawaii.

American Hawaii had the last two operating cruise ships built in the U.S. Most of the other domestically built ships in the industry had been scrapped, and demand for travel and tourism was increasing. So essentially, American Hawaii Cruises had a monopoly on the passenger cruise ship market among the Hawaiian Islands. And we could keep it if we could figure out how to build more ships in the U.S.

It was highly inefficient to construct these huge horizontal floating hotels on American soil because the only shipyards capable of the task were used solely by the military. Adapting them to build customized, consumer-oriented products was an ambitious program.

Our plan was to begin by refurbishing our two forty-plus-year-old existing ships and then follow with the construction of two new ones. The latter would be the first major cruise ships built domestically since the 1950s. We lobbied Congress, and the idea of boosting this sector in U.S. manufacturing caught on. Congress secured our loan guarantees, significantly reducing our cost of capital.

Ingalls Shipbuilding in Pascagoula, Mississippi, won the contract and began refurbishing our first ship. It was scheduled to begin service by late 2002, and the second ship was slated for 2004. The scenario positioned American Classic for a great decade of growth.

Then September 11 happened. Since American Classic's business was predicated on passengers flying to Hawaii to access our ships, the virtual halt in leisure air travel sank the company. Our shares plummeted, and American Classic was delisted. Our shareholders lost millions, as did the shipbuilders. I personally lost about $100 million. I'd taken the risk, but circumstances beyond my control intervened. It happens.

Incidentally, in 2000, I'd had the opportunity to bid on the World Trade Center. At the time Equity Office was the largest office building company in the U.S., and when the Port Authority of New York put the World Trade Center's lease up for bid, we were on top of the list. I sat down with Tim Callahan, who was the CEO of Equity Office at the time, and I told him this was another "hometown" deal. The effort to win it would be massive, with a small probability of winning. As an aside, I also mentioned that I didn't really want to own a target. Larry Silverstein won the bid and signed the lease for the World Trade Center in July 2001.

Tim was in San Francisco on September 11, and he didn't get home until the end of the week. He came to see me Friday morning at 7:00 a.m. "How did you know?" he asked. I said, "I didn't *know*, obviously, but terrorists attacked the World Trade Center in 1993. It was a symbol." It wasn't a bet I was willing to make.

American Classic wasn't the first, and it wouldn't be the last time I was blindsided by extraordinary events. In late 2006, I got an investment book marketing the 159-year-old Tribune Company. The media conglomerate was looking for a buyer, and it had an impressive portfolio of brands that together reached more than 80 percent of the households in the U.S.: major newspapers like the *Chicago Tribune*, the *LA Times*, the *Baltimore Sun*, and *New York Newsday*; superstation WGN America; twenty-three television stations, many of which were in strong markets; the TV Food Network, which had a solid following; a collection of promising Internet ventures, including cars.com and careerbuilder.com; and the Chicago Cubs, our beloved and profitable local team despite its stubborn losing record until 2016.

Many large private equity firms were interested in acquiring such strong brands—which is why I initially bowed out. A bidding war virtually guaranteed a higher sales price, so even if I won, I wouldn't get paid well enough to invest my time and best talent in the company. I don't like auctions, unless of course I'm running them. But one by one, the suitors began to drop out as the complexity of the company's troubles became clear. Tribune was a problem without an obvious solution—the kind of uncertainty that chases away traditional investors. It wasn't unique in that respect. Other large media companies were suffering from falling revenues as well. The onslaught of the Internet and its easy, free information and limitless advertising possibilities presented traditional media with an existential crisis—a question of identity that went to the heart of how the media industry would evolve in the decades ahead. Tribune's publishing business faced challenges, but the portfolio as a whole presented compelling opportunities that relied on executing change faster than the deterioration in traditional media.

A couple of months after I declined to bid, I got a call from one of Tribune's investment bankers. "The sales process has failed," he said. "There's no deal that makes sense." Then he asked me for a favor. "Can you go over to Tribune, take another look, and see if there's anything that can be done?"

So we took another look. Could we run it as a single entity without chopping it into pieces? I thought we could, although one piece would likely have to be monetized—the Chicago Cubs. It was not core to a media company, and we were confident it was a coveted asset for the right owner.

My parents, Rochelle and Bernard (shown here in their twenties), were my role models in doing the impossible. They escaped Nazi Poland for a new life in America.

Seen here in their forties, my parents became pillars of our Chicago community. My father always taught me that the most important thing I could have was *shem tov*—a good name.

Me, at around five. What else would an immigrants' kid growing up in the '40s want to dress up as?

By high school in 1955, I already had my first entrepreneurial venture—selling *Playboy* magazines to my friends at a substantial markup.

In 1963, I had just completed my BA and was headed to law school.

Bob Lurie was funny, colorful, analytical and a creative genius. He was the only true partner I ever had, and his friendship and input were irreplaceable.

Bob once jokingly wrote into a contract that any dispute would be settled by whoever was taller. Despite the angle of this photo, that dispute was never settled.

In the late 1980s, I handed out 8" x 10" copies of this photo at a meeting with bankers. It was my way of reassuring them about my level of commitment to recapitalize Apex Oil, which owned Clark retail gas stations. Sometimes a picture *is* worth a thousand words.

To me, motorcycles represent freedom. I take two trips a year with my friends, looking for twisty-turny roads around the world. We call ourselves the Zell's Angels.

Stopped for speeding in Poland, I tried to charm the police officer with one of the Santa Fe County, California sheriff patches we had brought along.

"The Emperor Has No Clothes" was the theme of my 1999 music box gift—my irreverent take on the dot com craze.

'FOR THE LAST TIME PENCIL NECK, IT'S NOT CALLED A TRAILER!'

My IPO roadshow T-shirts have always been playful but pointed. This one in 1993 challenged the negative stereotype about manufactured home communities.

The ducks—which I keep on the deck outside my office—in conference.

Photograph courtesy of the University of Michigan

Teaching a class at University of Michigan's Ross School of Business.

Photograph by Peter Ross

Having fun on the set of CNBC's *Squawk Box*.

Speaking at Chicago Ideas Week.

I ski like I live: I point my skis downhill and just go for it.

My wife, Helen, and I share a passion for surrealist and modern art.

A cartoon from my "little red book," which features some of my favorite sayings. I often hand it out as my business card.

Tribune was the ultimate challenge and opportunity. We saw myriad ways to unlock value through the company's diverse businesses. And that was intriguing now that nearly all the other bidders had left the room.

We offered a proposal to sponsor a going-private transaction by an employee stock ownership plan, or ESOP. Under the terms of the deal, all of the outstanding shares of Tribune would be acquired for cash through a multistep series of transactions. Upon completion, 100 percent of the company's stock would end up being held by the ESOP, which would be owned by company employees. So Tribune would be an employee-owned company.

We would invest roughly $315 million in the company in exchange for a $225 million subordinated promissory note and the right to buy about 40 percent of Tribune's equity in the future. Employees wouldn't be required to invest anything in the ESOP, and the new structure would shift all eligible employees to an ESOP stock-vesting schedule. The pension plan was already frozen for new hires and active only for grandfathered employees, so we would be creating a new retirement vehicle that included more employees as the company went forward. An independent entity—one of the most experienced ESOP trustees in the country—would represent employees in all the ESOP negotiations.

The ESOP structure would also unlock substantial value through immediate and long-term tax considerations. It would increase available cash by eliminating the need to pay taxes on ordinary income. This would save the company hundreds of millions of dollars, which could be used to address the debt service and operations. And after a ten-year holding period, the ESOP would not have to pay capital gains tax on hundreds of millions of dollars in asset appreciation.

The rub on the latter, of course, was the ten-year holding

period. The ESOP, the company, and any investors, including me, wouldn't realize these particular benefits for ten years. Few, if any, institutional investors wanted to wait around that long to realize the full upside from an investment. But I was a long-term holder. To me, Tribune was a strategic investment that I intended to hold for a very long time.

I had no interest in being a media mogul. I was a business guy, and as far as I was concerned, Tribune was a long-term business opportunity. That's the only way I ever looked at it.

There was certainly risk. But it could be mitigated, especially if all the employees were invested in the company's success. And Tribune's stock price was floundering after a failed sale process. Tribune had lost 46 percent of its market value from its peak two years earlier. The company's board was considering a number of highly leveraged transactions, in which money would be borrowed to pay shareholders a fair value on the assets.

Like many other going-private LBOs, our deal involved significant leverage. But ours had one big difference. If we succeeded in growing Tribune, many people would benefit, including, first and foremost, the employees. The ESOP would enable employees to participate in the upside. The majority of any increase in the value of the company's stock would accrue to the ESOP and ultimately to employees through their ESOP accounts. So employees would be highly motivated to succeed. That sounded great to me. Everyone would have skin in the game. Including me. It would be the single largest personal investment in my career.

I went in confident we would succeed. Combined with the immediate tax savings, my investment, and the prospective disposition of the Cubs, I believed we would have plenty of opportunity to improve the company's performance, first by growing the broadcast segments. Success was initially designed around a five-year strategy. Our plan was that by 2012, Tribune would have roughly 20 percent of its debt paid down and nearly half paid down within a decade. On April 1, 2007, the Tribune board accepted our bid—$34 a share in an $8.2 billion deal—and on December 20, we closed the deal.

Tribune was an institutional company with a hierarchical culture and dozens of business units that worked in silos. My vision was to open up the company's incredible platform, in essence to make both the parts and their sum as a whole stronger and more competitive through deep collaboration.

As we dug in, we heard a common phrase that sounded like a mantra: "We've just always done it that way." The phrase makes me shudder. To me it is the antithesis of progress. But beneath layers of bureaucracy, I saw employees with creativity, drive, and passion. I wanted to infuse them with an entrepreneurial spirit—to accelerate evolution through innovation, openness, and accountability. I knew that if I went into my new leadership role sounding like another Wall Street guy, I would just blend into the scenery. To galvanize employees, I chose a strong, outspoken approach. I knew that some of our strategies might not be popular, but I had never shied away from the heat of taking a company or industry in a new direction.

I also wanted to give employees a voice, to create a dialogue that could tap into the expertise embedded within the company. I have always prized leadership that isn't afraid to be challenged, that invites new ideas, and that seeks input from the employees on the ground. That was largely a new concept for employees at Tribune, and I wanted to hear what they had to say. One channel was through a direct email address, talktosam@tribune.com. I read and responded to every one of the hundreds of emails employees sent, and they were one of the highlights of my tenure at the company.

When we had proposed the transaction, we had factored in conservative assumptions. For instance, the rate of newspaper ad sales, which were a leading source of Tribune's revenue, was already in decline, but we underwrote the deal assuming a dramatically steeper drop. By all accounts we provided a healthy cushion for a worst-case scenario. Turned out, we would soon see unprecedented newspaper ad sale declines at levels no one had imagined. In the first quarter of 2008, just a few months after the deal closed, newspaper ad sale rates across the industry were multiples of the downside case we had assumed. Nine months later, by third quarter 2008, broadcast ad sales were historically bad too.

Of course the backdrop to our Tribune saga was the Great Recession. I don't think anyone envisioned how bad it was going to get. I certainly didn't. The financial crisis created a lending vacuum so potential buyers could not access capital, and there was no way for us to generate cash flow through asset dispositions.

These were desperate times. The long runway to execute our plan collapsed to a year or less. We fought to create a sense of urgency in an environment often defined by complacency. The company's whole ethos had to change if we were to have a chance of succeeding. It was tricky communicating this—a tightrope between motivation and a serious reality check. Employees and the unions were already nervous.

Within months of the closing, we were forced to drastically change our strategy in the face of massive declines in revenue. We hadn't planned on layoffs, but now we had to consider them. We hadn't planned to chop up the company's assets, but nothing was off the table. Instead of making investments in an evolutionary manner, we had to retrench. Tribune was going to have to become a much more nimble company.

We implemented what we called the 50/50 rule—50 percent content and 50 percent ads. The predictable outcome was that the papers were shrunk Mondays, Tuesdays, and Saturdays because there was less advertising demand. We also shrank the physical size of the newspapers by one inch. Those two changes translated into a roughly 15 percent reduction in the cost of producing the newspapers. In this case, 15 percent was a very big number. It equated to tens of millions of dollars in paper and ink alone.

These and other changes ignited a journalistic uproar. Some of the protests were against our placement of wraparound ads on the front page of the *LA Times*. Banner-wrap ads had never been done at Tribune before. The newsroom folks considered it a desecration. Today it's commonplace across the industry.

Every newspaper and broadcast station was run as if it was a stand-alone company. We looked at the numbers and saw that we had to begin cutting and reorganizing, starting with a 2 percent reduction in the workforce. And so the buyouts began. Personally, this was a very difficult message to deliver. I had stood with these people and promised growth. I had believed in the vision. I still did. But our backs were against the wall.

Simultaneously, we had to change the organization and structure of the newsrooms across the board. For example, in Fort Lauderdale, we had the *Sun Sentinel* and a TV station. So we moved the TV station into the *Sun Sentinel* building, creating a breaking news center that covered both TV and print. It was a simple move that introduced news coverage to the TV station without harming the product of the paper. And we looked for other opportunities like that across the company.

We were rigorous about examining ways to reduce redundancy. The papers had a tradition of jealously guarding their separate mastheads. For instance, the *LA Times* had a policy that no reporter could have a byline in the front section of the paper unless he or she was an *LA Times* employee. I thought that was a preposterous rule. If a story broke in Chicago, the home of Tribune, the *LA Times* would send a reporter, when instead the paper could have just called colleagues in Chicago to collaborate on the story. Similarly, the *Chicago Tribune* and the *LA Times* each sent foreign correspondents to Kabul for the *Afghan Idol* show. In effect, there were two stories—one with an *LA Times* byline and one with a *Chicago Tribune* byline, each talking about this great international event called *Afghan Idol*. It was an insane way to run a business.

Tribune's Washington bureau further epitomized the madness. Tribune had almost a hundred people there, representing the company's different newspapers, and they operated like they were competing entities rather than as mastheads under one umbrella. The *LA Times* even had its own separate entrance, as well as half the staff of the bureau. I called a meeting and told them a blunt truth. "We can't afford to have this kind of expense."

I asked them, "How many people here are from the *LA Times*?" They said forty-seven. I said, "So, you're telling me that a paper that represents 20 percent of the revenue of the company has almost half of the Washington bureau? That doesn't make any sense. You fix it or I will." They fixed it, but not without difficulty. They were so accustomed to being in the catbird seat that they didn't understand their part in the basic tenets of fiscal responsibility. They viewed me as an interloper, someone who didn't understand their business. But the facts were inescapable.

I got a lot of criticism for the way I tried to change Tribune—for the approach I used, as well as for the substance of the changes themselves. I know I used harsh language; I know my rhetoric was inflammatory. Most of it was deliberate. I wanted to ignite passion in the employees—to shake them out of the status quo, make them realize that they had to change, and help them do it. I didn't think I had all the answers. But it became increasingly obvious that without a serious wake-up call, Tribune—like all newspaper companies—would not succeed. The more stubborn the writers, editors, and executives got, the more agitated I became. It often seemed like they just didn't get it. Maybe I was too rough. But I wasn't wrong about where the business needed to go.

Regardless of all the issues swirling around us, we stayed focused and also turned our attention to accelerating revenue generation. We knew there had to be a way to monetize Tribune's established brands online, but its online division was a mess. The technology was antiquated, and every business used a different system and had no way to share data. There were disparate teams working on incompatible websites for the *Chicago Tribune* and the *LA Times*, and others working on hundreds of online projects, three-quarters of which wouldn't produce revenue for four to seven years. So we consolidated efforts and set clear priorities. There was a great deal of howling among the staff. There was a lot of flat-out denial about the extent—or the immediacy—of the crisis.

We had planned to keep all the newspapers. But the reality quickly became that we had to make some strategic dispositions. The one newspaper that everybody wanted was *Newsday* on Long Island. There were three leading bidders—Rupert Murdoch, owner of the News Corporation, including the *New York Post*; Mort Zuckerman, owner of the *Daily News*; and the Dolan family, owner of Cablevision. For Murdoch and Zuckerman, it was a no-brainer—a chance to consolidate influence and cut costs in the New York market. Cablevision's interest perplexed many observers, and for a while, it looked as if the company wasn't serious. But we believed if we could get them on board, Cablevision was the potential bidder that could pay us the most. So we were very disappointed when it seemed to be backing away, and it became increasingly clear that Murdoch was the most likely to come to the table with a deal.

The wrench in the works with a Murdoch deal revolved around the potential for cross-ownership and antitrust problems. We needed the cash and couldn't afford to be held up for a year and a half or more while the deal wound its way through the government bureaucracy. I knew that Murdoch had sidestepped that same problem with the *Wall Street Journal* by taking on the antitrust risk and guaranteeing the money up front. Was Murdoch willing to do the same for us?

Jimmy Lee, vice chairman of JPMorgan Chase and a master deal maker, was negotiating for Murdoch. The offer was a little low at $580 million, but doable. As we progressed, I kept telling him, "Everything is fine, but at this point, we've got to have a deal that works—and that means a guarantee." We went round and round, and it might have worked out eventually, but then someone leaked the details of the proposed $580 million deal, and suddenly I got a call from Chuck Dolan, founder and chairman of Cablevision. "I want to come to town and sit down with you," he said.

"Sure," I replied. "Come to lunch tomorrow." It looked like Cablevision was back in the game.

He showed up with his son James. They sat down and Chuck said, "We're interested in *Newsday*, and we're prepared to pay $650 million with no contingencies. So say yes, or say no." It was an easy decision—a no-contingency offer that was higher than

Murdoch's with no regulatory problems. We spent the weekend hashing out the details.

When Jimmy Lee heard, he was apoplectic. "They'll never close!" he screamed. "It won't happen!" He, of course, wanted his client to get the paper.

I said, "Jimmy, tell me how to solve the antitrust problem. This is more about certainty of closing than it is about the price."

He couldn't do it. With no antitrust issue and a $650 million all-cash offer, Cablevision was the winner.

It was a necessary cash infusion, but it wasn't enough.

We simply couldn't change course quickly enough. I hated to do it, but on December 9, 2008, just short of a year in, we filed Tribune for Chapter 11 bankruptcy protection. The filing gave the company breathing room to rework its debt.

I stayed on as chairman throughout the four-year bankruptcy process. We continued to invest our time, energy, and resources in the company—to make as much progress as we could under the bankruptcy restrictions. By the time Tribune emerged at the end of 2012 it was clear that the senior lenders who now owned the company felt (despite evidence to the contrary, including a rash of other bankruptcies across the industry) that only a media guy could fix things. I left them to it, but I disagreed with the premise. I think Tribune would have continued to benefit long-term from a fresh perspective. Certainly some of the "radical" initiatives we implemented are now commonplace within the industry.

I'm often asked if I regret doing the Tribune deal, if it was a bad deal, if I made a mistake with the ESOP. I don't see it that way. I made my best decision with the information I had available to me. I was fully invested in the company. Not just with capital, but with my time, which is much more important to me at this stage than money. I'm highly judicious about where I put my time—in terms of the opportunity cost of other deals I didn't do, and because time is my most valuable resource.

With Tribune, I saw the chance to transform an outdated operating model in a meaningful industry. To solve a problem. I believe our strategy was valid, and if we'd had more time, we could have made it work. We could have made a difference. In the end, that's what it comes down to for me. I often do the deals, take the risks that others won't because I believe I can make them work. And, frankly, I've got a long track record supporting that belief.

My whole life has been a progression of incremental insight into determining risks. Certainly when I think about the risks I took forty-five years ago, I think, "Yeesh, that was way too high." But based on what I knew at the time, I thought it was appropriate. Nothing refines your understanding and assessment of risk better than experience. But at any time, it's about being *aware* and simplifying the worst downside scenario—seeing over the abyss. It's about discipline and avoiding emotional response. And then you decide whether to play or walk.

As an entrepreneur, I am by nature an optimist. The word "failure" is not in my lexicon. I don't spend a lot of time lamenting on what could have been. My mental set is that my head doesn't turn all the way around. I am always compelled toward what is next.

My annual gift in 2009 summarized the year prior. It was an ode to our loss of Tribune and to the Great Recession, which, in addition to creating so much chaos for us, had devastated the financial and job markets and the banking and housing industries, and reset the growth expectations for the country.

Zero Visibility

The gift was titled "Zero Visibility," and, instead of my typical music box, it was a simple trifold board with the backdrop of the American flag. It included a pair of opaque sunglasses. It was the first time in fifteen years I delivered an annual gift with no music, and the first sentence of my accompanying note read "The music has stopped."

The following lyrics written to the tune of the national anthem were printed on the center trifold:

Oh say can you see, who turned out the lights?
The present is dark, the future ain't bright
Markets dazed and confused, sunk in crisis and fear
The gloom that has gathered is deep and severe
The search for quick answers, a task in futility
So what will succeed—how to foretell
Does our fate lie in the stars—or in ourselves?

I believe it is the latter.

CHAPTER NINE

Without Borders

In 2009, I read that Louis Vuitton and other high-end retailers were opening up stores in Mongolia. Huh? That got my attention. Mongolia had fewer than 3 million people, and over 700,000 of them were nomads. What would nomads need with Louis Vuitton? And Ulaanbaatar, Mongolia's largest city, was hardly world class. But Mongolia had begun development of one of the world's largest copper and gold deposits, the Oyu Tolgoi mine. It is well located to feed the insatiable commodity needs of China, whose border is about fifty miles away. The mine was expected to increase Mongolia's GDP by about 20 percent a year, and it was making a lot of Mongolians very rich.

So I went to Mongolia to check it out. When I got there, I met with the developer of Oyu Tolgoi and he took me on a tour. I was staggered by the scale of the undertaking. I'd been inclined to avoid the mining industry before, and this experience reaffirmed my attitude. The capital expenditure required to develop a mine that was 1.2 kilometers below the surface with a potential mineral supply of more than fifty years was daunting beyond belief—$10 billion just to bring the mine into production. I chose not to invest because of what happens at the end of every commodity cycle—more supply than demand.

It was a great trip, though, except for the food, which must be an acquired taste. After my first encounter with the smell of yak butter, which is a local staple, I restricted my diet to bananas and bread for the rest of my trip.

It shouldn't be surprising that, as the son of immigrants, I have an international orientation. Even as a young man, I was very interested in what was going on in the world and how events were relevant to my future. This wasn't just true in business. My innate curiosity also made me a world traveler. I'm intrigued by change and events surrounding it. Change leads to new experiences and opportunity. When I read or hear about a place that intrigues me, I go there. I've always been that way. But over the past twenty-five years in particular, I've made a concerted effort to see as much of the world as possible. Sometimes the impetus is a motorcycle trip, which lets me experience the landscapes and cultures close up. Other times it's an intriguing trend or anomaly—something I've read that piqued my curiosity as a potential business opportunity. Often it's both.

To me, everything is connected. I believe that globalization provides more opportunity than threat. The days when demand was created only within our own borders are over. Today, you can draw lines between demand for apartments in the U.S. and world trade flows, international currencies, and perspectives of stability in other countries. I don't think we've even begun to understand the various ways that interconnection and interdependency will evolve over the next couple of decades.

Being global, if not in business then in mind-set, isn't really a choice, in my opinion. It's a mandate, a responsibility, and a thrill. So, in the late 1990s, I turned my business interests to the international markets in earnest with the creation of another private investment firm, Equity International.

By then we had spun out our U.S. commercial real estate portfolios into public companies, and I was a full believer in the value of liquid real estate. The industry was on the verge of unprecedented monetization, growth, and scale in the States. Our companies had access to capital in ways we had never imagined. It was revolutionary. I knew the same potential existed in other countries, and my experience in the U.S. would give me an advantage.

Once again, I listened as people told me I was nuts. Emerging markets were largely considered untouchable by foreign investors at the time. They were still under the shadow of loan defaults from the 1980s, and Mexico's recent Tequila Crisis (the devaluation of the peso) had triggered widespread currency devaluation across Latin America. To top it off, many emerging market countries were reeling from the Asian financial crisis in 1997 and Russia's default in 1998. Emerging markets at the time were not for the faint of heart. For me, of course, that presented an environment with no competition for assets. It was an exciting new world of opportunity.

I believed that the fundamentals of real estate were universal. That is, issues of supply and demand, demographics, capital flows, and so on were as relevant overseas as they were here at home. But our first thesis for international investing lasted only a few months. Seeing potential opportunities is one thing; knowing how to take advantage of them is another.

Our first efforts offshore reflected the strategy we had employed in the U.S. We would invest in properties and create a holding company "mother ship" as the owner of assets. Our larger goal would be to bring that company to the public markets. After making a few international investments with our own capital, however, it became obvious that institutional investors would not be able (or willing) to follow the cross-border complexities involved with a REIT that had assets in many different countries. The varying country tax codes and currencies would make the REIT nontransparent and less predictable—which was exactly the opposite of what I'd worked so hard to achieve in the U.S.

To add to the problem, ownership of commercial real estate in emerging markets back then was very complex. Most buildings were owner-occupied, which could mean hundreds of owners for just one office building. These markets didn't have pools of investment capital for real estate projects, and developers couldn't afford to hold their new buildings until they leased up. They had to sell space floor by floor or unit by unit to end users or small investors as a way to recirculate capital for their next project. But demand for leased space was growing as more multinational companies entered emerging market countries. Multinationals were not used to, nor were they interested in, owning their own space.

So we refocused on investing in real estate companies rather than in properties—a strategy that had worked well for us in other industries, like manufacturing. Our thesis worked and literally a world of opportunity opened up to us.

It also opened up new challenges. When you invest in emerging markets, you're trading the rule of law for growth. If you think you can count on receiving justice in a foreign courtroom, you should think again. So, the first question is always "Who's your partner?" By that I mean "Who is going to watch your interests on the ground every day?"

We look for partners in-country to invest alongside us—people we trust, whose interests align with ours, who are like-minded and believe in transparency and long-term relationships. We want a savvy, committed ally—someone who responds favorably when we say "We believe in you, we'll make this happen. How can we support you? How can we help you?" They are as engaged as we are, and they understand that they'll prosper along with us. Their knowledge of the way things work locally is critical, and their affiliations often take us further than any foreigner could go on the upside while preventing us from falling too far on the downside.

Take our investment in Venezuela early in the Chavez regime. It was in a company that owned one of the largest first-class office building portfolios in Latin America. It had a great multinational tenant roster, from Exxon to Citigroup, and was poised for growth throughout the region. In early 2004, as Chavez's rhetoric about the government's reach increased, our local partner said, "Don't worry about what he says; worry about what he does." Then, later that year, our partner called us and said, "Chavez is starting to take action. Now it's time to worry." It was a mad rush to the exit, and we weren't the only ones scrambling. But because we had a great partner on the ground, we were able to sell our position soon after. It was at a loss, but a much better outcome than if we hadn't had his local expertise and influence.

So we focus on finding great partners—local developers and operators—and we help them create institutional-quality operating platforms to develop, own, and lease large portfolios of commercial real estate. We look for businesses with the potential for growth so that ultimately we can create value from more than just bricks and mortar. We infuse our portfolio companies with capital and guide them in deploying it, and we help them become institutional grade by teaching them strong fiscal discipline and corporate governance, lending our expertise in sophisticated investing and business strategies, sharing our knowledge of public markets, and introducing them to our network of banking and other relationships. Together we form that 1 + 1 = 3 equation.

A great example of this type of partnership, as well as of the consolidation opportunities in emerging markets, is BR Malls in Brazil. In the early 2000s, new malls were sprouting up all over São Paulo and Rio, and industry ownership, as I've mentioned, was highly fragmented. We partnered with a local private equity firm to create BR Malls as a growth platform in 2006, investing $86 million. Roughly a year later, we led BR Malls in an IPO on Brazil's Bovespa at an equity valuation of roughly R$2.1 billion. The capital enabled BR Malls to lead the industry in acquisitions. Five years later, the company had nearly fifty malls. Total returns for public shareholders were over 26 percent, and BR Malls had an equity market cap of R$10.7 billion. By the time we fully exited the investment in 2010, BR Malls was the largest mall company in Brazil, and we had achieved a 4.2x multiple, or 48.6 percent IRR.

This is our primary premise in international investing—the transformation of businesses into institutional platforms. We started in Mexico, then went to Brazil. Then to Colombia, India, and China. So far we've brought about thirty companies in fifteen countries along for the ride, with four IPOs.

I'm drawn to emerging markets because of their built-in demand. I've always believed in buying into in-place demand rather than trying to create it. To me, international investing is largely a story of demography. Just look at population growth. Most of the developed countries (e.g., U.K., France, Japan, Spain, Italy) have aging populations and are ending each year with flat or negative population growth rates. For instance, we don't spend much time looking at Western Europe. It's Disneyland. It's great for wine and castles and cheese, but there's no growth there. Further, Europe has the largest population of pensioners in the world. The number of retirees who don't work is close to double what we have in the U.S. and most of those European countries fund each year's pensions from taxes. It begs the question, with a shrinking workforce where will that money come from?

In contrast, most of the emerging markets (e.g., India, Mexico, Colombia, South Africa, Brazil) have younger populations and higher growth rates. And while growth rates across the board have fallen off a cliff since 2007, emerging markets are still ahead of developed countries. That means more built-in demand.

In the early 2000s, demographic trends and fiscal discipline in several emerging markets were rapidly increasing the size of their respective middle classes. I knew that growth would generate demand for housing, retail, and other real estate. So we looked for opportunities in that arena.

In addition to demographics, we look at national stability. Political leadership is particularly important in the rapidly changing environments of emerging markets. The ideal is a growth-oriented president who is a fiscal conservative and a social liberal—someone who governs from the middle.

Brazil is a great example of the impact of leadership—both good and bad—and with the same president. Brazilian president Lula, who was elected in 2002, followed his predecessor's economic model of a macro tripod—maintaining a fiscal surplus, targeting inflation, and instituting floating exchange rates. Basically, Lula stayed out of the way of growth. He paid down Brazil's deficit and capped inflation. As a result, the country was able to secure an investment-grade rating and fully benefit from ten years of strong export growth and a strong global economy. The Brazilian real got stronger and, with Lula's lack of interference, the new middle class emerged. But in his second term, Lula's discipline eroded, and by the time he left office, a great deal of the progress had been wasted.

Lula's successor was Dilma Rousseff, who had been in his cabinet. She proved to be a heavy-handed leader who continued to introduce intrusive state-led initiatives and set policies and regulations that crippled most private businesses by picking state-owned and privileged companies as "winners" deserving of subsidies and easy credit. The close ties the government had with these companies bred an environment ripe for misuse. She also doubled Brazil's deficit within three years. The Petrobras corruption scandal didn't come as a surprise, but its size and scale did. Rousseff's corrupt leadership cast a black cloud over the whole country. She destroyed the confidence of institutional investors and made Brazil a pariah in the international investing community. Investors competing for deals in Brazil fled the market.

Brazil is now trying to get back on track. To fully recover, the country will have to acknowledge incurred losses and implement reforms that encourage growth and lessen government interference. But the basics—self-sufficiency in food and energy, and scale to grow—give me the conviction that, in the long term, the country has a promising future.

You can't talk about the impact of government leadership or politics on a country's economy without talking about China. Where Brazil and Mexico are more market-oriented economies, China is more of a command economy. In China, the rules under which you invest can change at the whim of the government. There is less predictability and assurance in China than in any other major world economy. But it's so large, you can't ignore the opportunity. People always say that to be successful, all you need is demand from 1 percent of China's 1.4 billion population. To me, the discount in pricing has to be exceptionally higher to warrant the additional risk.

In 2006, China was suffering from a dearth of available investment capital. Locals were waving in U.S. and other foreign investors with open arms. As you know by now, I love a market or deal that is starved for investors. It creates an environment where sellers and partners are bending over backward for you. I discovered that advantage over and over in my career, and I'm always on the lookout for that dynamic.

So we invested in a Chinese home builder, based largely on the market need for capital and the premise of a robust government mortgage program. Our partner was fully bilingual in English and Mandarin. Everything was great. Over the next two years, the Chinese housing market grew, the Shanghai Stock Exchange was on the rebound, and the country regained a robust access to capital. And then overnight, the government killed the mortgage program without warning. And our partner forgot how to speak English. He just stopped communicating with us entirely. The bottom line was he didn't need our money anymore. This experience reaffirmed my basic tenet that global markets require good partners, aligned interests, and common objectives. Although we liquidated our position at a profit, the effort in and out was not worth the result.

In emerging markets, a big clue to national stability is whether a country is on the verge of investment-grade rating. Early on, I came to the conclusion there's no other time in the life of any country when it's more disciplined and more transparent than when it's a year or two away from reaching investment-grade status. The ranking translates into an immediate benefit for a country, so it's on its best behavior. Investment grade strengthens the country's currency, leads to increased demand for investment opportunities from foreign direct investors, boosts world confidence in the economy—because the country has demonstrated discipline within the political system—and rewards the country with a lower cost and greater access to capital. We invested in Mexico, Brazil, and Colombia when each was on the verge of investment grade, and we benefited from this impact firsthand.

Some emerging markets will check all the boxes—strong population growth, growing middle class, verge of investment grade, great leadership, and hunger for capital—and then be missing the one ingredient that enables you to monetize your investment: scale. Without scale, you don't have liquidity. You have no optionality. In essence, you're stuck. Africa is a great example. I think many countries, such as Botswana, have potential, but the upper and middle classes are too small for me to get involved. Chile is another example. It has the institutions and leadership, but only 17 million people—no scale.

Of all the corners of the world, I believe Latin America has some of the best investment opportunities for the next decade at least. The creation of the Mercado Integrado Latinoamericano (MILA) in 2011, which combined the stock exchanges of Colombia, Peru, and Chile, and Mexico a few years later, infused the region with liquidity and will continue to accelerate its growth. India is also interesting but has a history of disappointing international investors. It's a hard place to do business, but we believe there is opportunity there as well.

In particular, we are drawn to Mexico. After the Fukushima nuclear disaster occurred in Japan in 2011, nearly every multinational executive I talked to was bemoaning the cost of delays and availabilities in exports coming out of Asia. I couldn't help but think that companies would not want to get caught in that type of scenario again, so they would be looking for an alternative manufacturing option closer to home. The only logical place was Mexico. Also, Chinese labor costs were steadily rising and eroding the margin for U.S. companies to manufacture there. So we invested in a Mexican warehouse and logistics company to support what I believed to be a pretty good bet on future growth. Sure enough, within four years, Mexico was in a manufacturing boom with a double-digit increase in exports from Mexican factories.

We continue to view opportunity on a global scale. I see international investing as a challenge of connecting multiple dots to reach a conclusion. My job has always been to identify the dots we should pay attention to as well as the incentives that will connect them—all to get maximum possible results.

I've mentioned before that I love meeting people on their own turf. But in foreign markets, that takes on a whole new depth. In my experience, you tend to spend more time together when you're a guest. And the conversations range broader and go deeper. You talk about investment opportunities, sure, but also about world affairs and local relationships and culture, about what they think of America, current events, and other topics. To my amazement, people share their thoughts in a remarkably candid way. I simply love it.

I've always valued long-term relationships, but John Hsieh, the former head of Itel's container leasing business, taught me that you simply cannot succeed in-country without them. Hsieh had extensive international experience and contacts. He took me under his wing, and we traveled the world meeting Itel's customers and suppliers—from a cocktail party in Rotterdam with British and German customers to a dinner in Hong Kong with a

Chinese shipping company. The deep relationships he had with his customers enlightened me. I learned that the extreme degree to which you rely on strong personal relationships is perhaps the single biggest difference between doing business in the emerging markets and the U.S.

And where those connections can lead me is fascinating—to unprecedented deals, lifelong friendships, and unforgettable experiences. Sometimes a deal will make a lasting impact. Here's an example.

Over the years, I did business and became fast friends with Juan Gallardo, the chairman and CEO of a large Mexican sugar and beverage company. In 2008, he brought me a crazy idea. He and some other private investors from Mexico wanted to build a pedestrian bridge across the U.S.–Mexico border that would physically connect a new building in the southernmost part of San Diego directly with the Tijuana International Airport, which, by an accident of geography, sits just five hundred feet south of the States. Nothing like it existed. Turns out more than 2 million people already cross the border back and forth to fly in or out of the airport. And passengers who used the existing border crossings had to take a circuitous route through Tijuana to get there and then wait hours to cross. There was built-in demand.

So we jumped in, and our team led an eight-year approval process, working with Homeland Security and a slew of other U.S. government agencies, to make it happen. Cross Border Xpress (CBX) opened in December 2015 and is already accelerating travel, tourism, and commerce in the Baja/California regional economy. It promotes opportunity. And to me, that is what it's all about. As I said at the press conference for the opening, "While some people are trying to build a wall, I've built a bridge."

Our activity in Mexico also connected me to the United Arab

Emirates. Our success with an investment in Mexico led to an inquiry from the Royal Family, and I met with them and the Crown Prince of Abu Dhabi in 2005. That too has evolved into a great friendship for me.

As Americans, we sometimes have a tendency to stereotype people from cultures we don't understand, and this is especially true of the Middle East. The prince, having studied in the United States, was known to be committed to improving the Emirates' relationships in the West—both politically and financially. When he heard about our work in Mexico and low-income housing, he invited me to visit. Abu Dhabi was growing rapidly, and housing for the expanding labor force was a priority.

During our first meeting, I said, "I was told that you ride motorcycles."

He smiled and said yes.

"Well, I would love to go for a ride with you, if that's possible while I'm here."

He said, "How about tomorrow night?"

I was delighted. The next night, at 11:00 p.m., I went to his complex and there were ten motorcycles lined up. "Pick whichever one you like," he offered. I chose a Ducati 1000, and he rode a Triumph.

We rode all over Abu Dhabi, and it was a wonderful experience, just beautiful. At one point, we came up to a stoplight and a car pulled alongside us. The driver and his passenger gaped out the window. I'm sure they had quite a story to tell their friends. Their ruler flying along on a motorcycle! When I mentioned the driver's reaction, the prince laughed and told me it was one reason he only rode at night. When he tried it during the day, everything came to a standstill.

I've always enjoyed seeing the great pride people have in their countries and how eager they are to show them off. Among the most memorable trips for me was a helicopter ride over the eerie tepuis (or tabletop) mountains, hosted by my partner in Venezuela. Three hundred fifty miles southeast of Caracas and reachable only by air or a three-day hike, the tepuis are mountains inexplicably sheared off at the tops. There are about a hundred of these mountains, and they appear out of the jungle like giant candles. They are like massive tables with sheer cliffs on all sides. Some of the mountains are almost ten thousand feet high, and among them is Mount Roraima, said to be one of the oldest geological formations on Earth—over two billion years old. We spent the day flying in and out, around and below these ancient, mammoth structures. We landed at both the top and the bottom of Angel Falls, the world's highest uninterrupted waterfall, and then we lunched in a remote Indian village. It was one of the most exciting and memorable things I've ever done.

I'm especially intrigued to see places that have been closed to travelers for years. In 2004, when the U.S. normalized relations with Libya, the country opened up to passenger air travel, among other things. So my wife, Helen, and I planned a trip, along with my sister Julie and her husband, Roger. Through my connection in the United Arab Emirates, I had met a businessman from Libya, and he invited us to visit. Upon landing in Tripoli, the capital, we discovered that immigration and customs were not relevant. Our car just drove right up to the plane, we climbed in, and that was it. No checkpoint. No nothing.

The real attraction of the trip was the Old Town of Ghadames, which was built over twenty-five hundred years ago. Constructed out of mud and limestone, Ghadames was built in layers, essentially creating a covered city. The lower layer was a labyrinth of tunneled passages; the only light came from ventilation holes that emitted a little sunlight and mirrors that reflected it. The clever architecture protected residents from the desert heat. The second layer aboveground was a roofless network of pathways. It was an entirely self-sufficient society, with a complex irrigation system, working sewers, a thriving economy, and trade with aboveground societies. Amazingly, it was fully inhabited until the mid-1980s, when Libya built housing nearby and encouraged residents to move on the pretext that modern housing was more humane. But residents didn't want to leave, and the last family didn't move out until the late 1990s. Just extraordinary.

On another trip in the mid-1990s, we were in the Far East and had to stop for fuel on the Kamchatka Peninsula, which was known as the location of top-secret Soviet Union military installations. Landing at the old airport was eerie. The runway was overgrown, with grass coming out of every crevice, and on either side were bunkers and hangers where military helicopters and jets still sat. It all looked as if it had been abandoned for years, and I guess it had been. It was like the last gasp of the Cold War—a shadow reminder.

When you're hungry for experience, you just get to do more—even when it's out of character. Like when I went turkey hunting in Morocco. By choice, I was the only guy without a gun. What's a nice Jewish guy going to do with a gun? I was worried I might inadvertently shoot someone.

Getting to embed yourself in the culture *is* the experience. But sometimes it takes you a little closer than you want to be. In the mid-1990s, for one of our Zell's Angels trips, we went to Eastern Europe. We started in Prague and left the next day for Krakow, about a five-and-a-half-hour ride. Headed to the Polish border, we were on the expressway the Soviets used in the 1960s to invade Czechoslovakia, and a couple of us got stopped by the cops for speeding. We, of course, attempted to talk our way out of it, which was difficult with a conversation in two different languages. At this point, I should tell you that for every bike trip, we always have a custom T-shirt, hat, or sweatshirt listing the cities we are visiting. And we always carry extras. This trip's shirt was vomit green. Don't ask me why. So when negotiations with the cop who stopped us seemed to be failing, we suggested that maybe he'd like a Western souvenir as a gift. We pulled it out. He paused. And then he looked at us and said in broken English, "Don't you have another color?"

Later, when we crossed into Poland, there were two police officers along the side of the road holding white wands. They waved their wands at us, and we waved back. Ten minutes later, I looked in my rearview mirror and saw that a police officer had one of our guys stopped and was holding a gun to his head. Unbeknownst to us, in Poland, when the police wave white wands, you're supposed to pull over. But we had a secret weapon. One of our riders was an honorary sheriff, and he always brought a supply of sheriff's patches with the American flag on every trip. He would trade them for memorabilia like belts and buttons of the local police. And that's how we got a pass for not stopping for the border guards.

All of it—the travel, the friendships, the deals, the partners—has given me a better orientation to the world around me. And from that I have a better understanding of how I can participate—not just out there, but back home too.

CHAPTER TEN

Behind the Deals

I often say I'm chairman of everything and the CEO of nothing. I stick to what I'm good at—vision, direction, strategy. That's where I add the most value. I spend almost my entire day listening to other people. I ask questions, I probe, I raise possibilities.

My world, the Equity world, stretches well beyond the private investment firm I started nearly fifty years ago. It includes all of the various Equity-named companies I've started since—five in all—as well as the companies I chair or influence with a significant ownership stake. I pick great people to run them. I don't involve myself in the day-to-day, but I stay close to those who do.

I believe in the radius theory of business, where your ability to succeed is ultimately limited by the number of people between you and the decision. That's because the farther from you the decision is made, the less you control the risk. History shows that businesses get buried when they don't delegate enough—but also when they delegate too much.

From the early days of building my firm with Bob Lurie and throughout the growth of my business, I've always kept one thing at the forefront: the idea that culture is king. The environment you spend most of your waking hours in reflects who you are and the type of people you want working with and for you. Culture can either inspire ideas or stifle them. It can lay the basis for relationships that last decades or flip through them like a deck of cards. It is the heartbeat of your company.

So I want to talk a bit about our culture because I credit so much of my success to it.

At our core, we are a meritocracy—an environment that Bob and I cultivated in the early days. A meritocracy gives you the freedom to be yourself by eliminating superficial markers, so you are measured only by what you produce. In essence, it is an equalizer that focuses everybody on what's important so you have the opportunity to reveal your best. Once you've worked in a true meritocracy, it's very hard to settle for anything else.

Beyond that, our culture is driven, creative, playful, effective, and smart. We encourage confidence and nurture the ability for you to have an opinion—and to back it up intelligently. I also often say we have an "open kimono" policy. No secrets, no whispers, no closed doors. Everything is on full display. That's one of the key ways we manage risk.

Sometimes this policy is tangible. I'll give you an example of what I mean. I've had the same office for thirty-five years, and just four years ago, during a renovation, I discovered that it had a door. I never knew it was there because it's a pocket door and it had never been closed once in all those years.

Everyone is welcome in my office, from senior executives to the person in the mailroom. By extension, if the number one guy is totally accessible, then anyone else who isn't looks like a schmuck. None of my people work closeted in their offices.

By contrast, I once visited the offices of a well-known architect in Los Angeles. His operation was set up so that there was a series of glass offices for the executives on the window line, then a series of interior secretarial desks, and his office was at the end in the corner. So I was standing there one day talking to his secretary. She told me, "You know, my boss asks me how I am every day as he walks by, but by the time I answer him he's already in his office." And I just looked at her and said, "Well, it's really hard to stop when you're walking on water."

We weed that behavior out in my company. Be prepared to be kidded, be prepared to have your ideas challenged, and plan on staying connected—with everyone.

As a risk-taker, my greatest fear is not having information that might protect me from making a mistake. The only way I can do that is to create an atmosphere where there are no silos—where everybody knows everything that's going on. I tell people "No surprises" and I mean it. I'm confident enough to believe that if I catch a problem early on, we'll be smart enough to fix it. So, *don't hide things. Relax. We don't kill the messenger around here.*

At the same time, I run an entrepreneurial organization. I *empower* people. I love self-starters. I want people taking the initiative, pushing the edge, questioning, challenging. Of course, that kind of freedom comes with responsibility, so good judgment is critical. Fortunately, I've always been a pretty good judge of talent.

A lot of the trust I have in my team has to do with my hiring process. It can be a little unusual. When I'm looking for a senior person, I don't write a job description and then look for someone to fit it. I find talented people who fit my organization and then look for ways to use them. Most of the time that system works as expected. When occasionally it doesn't, it's abundantly clear.

A number of years ago, I hired a brilliant woman who had

worked for some of the biggest companies in the world. Six months into her tenure, I fired her. Why? She was political. She'd come up in a culture that used information as currency. She hoarded it while she tried to work angles. I don't blame her for being that way; hell, many businesses operate on the law of the jungle—one person's survival is dependent on another's failure. She might have been brilliant in that world, but in my culture she didn't fit because here we share. Secrets are what bury you. I'm sure this remarkable woman had never been fired before in her life. I'm sure she's gone on to have a great career, but the concept of using information as leverage just doesn't work for me.

There's a baseline IQ level needed to work at my firm, but I don't need rocket scientists. After that, what best predicts your success in my world is drive, energy, attitude, judgment, conviction, and passion. And an ability to cut to the center of an issue. I'd trade another twenty IQ points for those qualities any day. I've had a number of brilliant people working for me who didn't make it because they couldn't grasp how to think about a deal. I remember walking into the office one night around 8:00 p.m. to find a guy working on a ten-year projection for a real estate project we were considering buying. I looked at what he was doing and I realized how many hours he'd spent laboring over his calculations. His approach was ass-backward. I said, "You've got to be able to look at the deal and know what it hinges on to know whether it works or not. If you realize that the key component works, then you use the numbers to test it. You don't do the numbers to find out eight hours later whether it was worth starting." I'm sure his IQ was higher than mine. But that isn't how we operate. You have to be able to effectively assess the initial picture and see where the greatest risk is most likely to be, or you'll spend your life doing numbers just to find out if a deal will work.

And all that time lost is time you could have been looking at other opportunities.

I constantly challenge my people to "take me on." I want them to challenge me just like I'm challenging them. We should both be able to succinctly defend our positions on any deal. It just makes us all smarter. I'm getting the most out of them, and they're getting the most out of me. Win-win.

Increasingly over the past twenty to thirty years, I've had to try to get people to *not* treat me like the boss. To let their guard down so ideas can flow. Don't get me wrong. I like being the boss. I accept the responsibility and I've done very well with it, but I don't want to be surrounded by sycophants. The worst thing for me would be an environment where everybody just said, "Okay, Sam, whatever you say" all the time. That would be death in an entrepreneurial environment. I tell people, "Don't parrot back to me what I think, and don't try to guess what I think. I want to know what *you* think." And I do that over and over again until the right answer pops out. When I sit in my office with a group of people, I don't seek deference; I seek ideas. In that setting, every person is on a level playing field. They also each have a stake in every endeavor.

By now you know I'm a great believer in aligned interests—skin in the game. From the very first deals we did at EGI, I have spread the opportunity—both the risks and the rewards. We co-invest, side by side, and I often provide a "promote" to my people, allowing them to share in profits on a portion of my invested capital. That means I put my money behind theirs (say $150,000 of my money to $30,000 of their money), and if our investments or funds achieve their minimum target metrics, my people get returns based on the aggregate ($180,000). In effect, we're all invested in each other's success. It's not only about motivation; it's a mandate to collaborate. Deal opportunities and challenges are discussed, questioned, and probed by the team at large because everybody has a piece of everybody else's deal. There isn't anything that turns me on more than the fact that I've created thousands of jobs and seemingly limitless opportunity for my employees. And that I've made hundreds of millionaires. I don't just pay lip service to the idea that you can prosper on my team.

So, my executives don't create fiefdoms. We may have some internal rivalries, but they come second to furthering the greater good. This collaborative culture extends beyond my private investment firm to the various companies I chair, own, or have a significant stake in. It can be astonishing to watch it in action. We have some of the most skilled and competitive executives in the world, and every single day you'll find examples of them dropping what they're doing to help the other guy. Executives in my network have access to vast resources and a wide range of peers who make them instantly smarter and faster on nearly every subject. Add to that the thousands of alumni who have worked within our world for more than forty-five years, and you get a sense of the power behind our culture.

I have a pretty good radar on people. Once I decide I trust you, I back it up by giving you a lot of responsibility quickly. I'll take a risk with you. (Like Jay Pritzker did with me.) If I'm right, you'll work incredibly hard to prove—to me and yourself—that you're up to the challenge. You get a chance to stretch in ways you likely haven't before. It's addictive, and I've been told it engenders fierce loyalty. And that loyalty goes both ways.

I tell people who join my company, "Once you work for us, you're never going to be happy working anywhere else." And I believe it's true. We have people who never leave, and many who do try to come back. The length of tenure for our employees is unusual; many of my people have been with me for twenty- or thirty-plus years—from my assistant to middle managers to CEOs. There's always new opportunity here. Every time we change direction, we create new ways for people to grow. You'll often see our employees moving from one Equity company to another for a new position that gives them that chance.

One of the very few senior managers who ever voluntarily left ended up coming back. He'd left after twenty years for a job that paid more money and gave him more power, so when he returned I was curious to know why. "I don't understand," I said. "You were earning twice as much money, you had a much higher position. Why did you come back?"

He said, "It's really simple. When I was here, if I had a problem, I walked down to your office and asked you the question— and you'd answer it. I had instant access. In my new company, every issue involved writing memos to half a dozen people, and by the time we got to the end, all creativity had been stifled. You could hardly remember the idea you started with." Fast decision making and autonomy had become like oxygen to him.

As another example, we recently had to establish, from scratch, an entirely new management team for a $6 billion office company in just a few months. We were flooded with calls from people who had worked for Equity Office before we sold it, or who had been with one of our other Equity companies. Within weeks, we had thirty employees up and running, and twenty-six of them were from our Equity family of companies.

The creative expressions of who we are as a firm and who I am as a person often overlap.

We're irreverent and not above poking fun—at ourselves, at each other, and particularly at bureaucrats, who are depicted in our offices in sculptures sitting in boiling oil, bound in reams of red tape, and doing the bureaucratic shuffle. I encourage the occasional Ping-Pong tournament or game of bag toss out on the deck and, hopefully, the annual mimosa party to watch the Blackhawks' Stanley Cup parade. But of course to me, perks don't make the work fun. The work does.

One of the secrets to having fun that people often don't appreciate is that in the midst of it you can be pretty profound. I am a big believer in the art of communication. It's everything. But communication isn't always with words, and a message doesn't have to be sober and dry to be effective.

I am at heart a salesman, and most of all I like selling ideas. I try to make memorable points about a deal, the economy, whatever, and at the same time convey that we at Equity are different.

While I began tapping into my creative vein early on, a guy named Peter Szollosi helped me take it to a whole new level. I met Peter on a motorcycle trip in Colorado in 1988. Peter was a creative genius. He had a mind that just saw the world from a different perspective. There were no limits to his thinking that I was ever able to detect. Peter had his own graphics design firm in Denver doing one-off projects and pretty much running in place. When we met, I didn't have clarity on what we would accomplish together, but I thought the potential was great.

I knew that if we could create a brand or following in the public markets, we would be able to monetize it. So I invited Peter to Chicago and we sat down in my office. I showed him a few of my early concepts and discussed how we might use year-end gifts and other off-the-wall ideas to remind people that when they did business with us, they were interacting with someone *different.* Then I asked him, "Would you like to come here and take over the creative work?" I said I didn't yet know whether it would be a full-time job but added, "You've got nothing better to do, so come do this." And he did. Not only did it turn into a full-time job, but in time it became a whole department, which still represents a core element of our company culture to this day. Peter got his dream job, and I got the creative heartbeat of my company. Under Peter's leadership we began imparting our vision to the world in clever, often irreverent ways—T-shirts that capture the key message for an IPO or annual gifts that convey a driving economic theme for the coming year.

Sadly, we lost Peter to cancer in 2007. It was a personal and professional blow unlike any since losing Bob. His vision for the creative department he built lives on though with the leadership of his successor and close friend, Bill Bartolotta.

One of their projects was creating my "business card"—a little red book of Samisms that I feel have particular meaning. "Trying to be right 100 percent of the time leads to paralysis" goes one. "Conventional wisdom is nothing other than a reference point" is another. And my favorite, "Am I being too subtle?" Of course, each is accompanied with a cartoon.

Finally, every two or three years, I host a party for my birthday and invite about eight hundred people. I don't care about my birthday, but it's an excuse to get my network of people together at a creative, unforgettable event. The parties began in the late 1960s as treasure hunts, an idea that originated from my experience at Camp Ramah, the Jewish summer camp I attended as a kid. There, the clues were based on biblical verses that progressively identified locations on the campground until you progressed to the end. For my parties, rather than use the

Bible, I picked different themes each year to lead guests to locations throughout Chicago. One year it was hospitals, another it was hotels, another it was charitable institutions, and so on. Each team would get a list of a hundred potential locations, so that the playing field would be fair for out-of-towners. The clues went something like this: for a church, the clue was "No poke folk," and the answer was Immaculate Conception Church. For a building, it was "Monopoly," and the answer was Board of Trade. For municipal facilities, a clue was "Beaver power," and the answer was Voltz Road Dam. And so on.

At each event, the guests were assigned to teams and sent off in groups of about six in limos to terrorize the city. There was no prize, except for braggers' rights, which in my crowd was actually a great incentive.

When a team would get stuck, they'd call in. I'd be sitting by the phone drinking wine, and I'd have a great time berating them before giving them an additional hint.

These treasure hunts were an adaptation of how we work in business, even today. I see a trend or anomaly, outline a general direction, and say, "Let's go." My people get together and debate all the variations that direction could mean, and then they go off and try to prove they are right in their particular interpretation. It is an R&D approach to opportunity. And it creates a healthy internal competition, a charge in the atmosphere where everyone is propelled by the other to do their best. At the same time, as I've mentioned, everybody shares the spoils and risks of whichever deal wins the day. So even if your deal isn't picked, you want the other person's to succeed.

Meanwhile, if someone gets stuck in the process, they circle back with me. Of course with the treasure hunts, I knew all the answers and there wasn't millions at stake. At work, we puzzle through the obstacles together, and then I set the next milestone.

I give my people a lot of freedom to explore and problem solve while I control the risk through big decisions. This autonomy, coupled with the access to fast decisions, is like crack to my people. They know I trust them. I don't say it. I *show* it. When I put millions behind a deal one of my investment people sourced, researched, negotiated, and closed, it creates an electric, exhilarating environment.

Anyway, after twenty-six years, the size of the treasure hunts grew from thirty players to 240. At that point, the logistics overcame our ability to execute effectively, and that's when I switched from treasure hunts to treasured events.

Switching the parties to a single location upped the creative challenge. My goal became to create a complex, creative, mind-stretching experience that was virtually impossible to describe the next day. Or if you *could* get a description, it would be vastly different from one guest's to the next. We'd also feature headliner entertainment like Elton John, Jay Leno, Bette Midler, the Eagles, the Beach Boys, Fleetwood Mac, Aretha Franklin, James Brown, and Cirque du Soleil. One my favorites was in 2006. It began with guests boarding boats that took them to a boatyard near the Indiana–Illinois border. We had assembled 450 oceangoing shipping containers, each of which weighed about four tons, into a 35,000-square-foot venue. Doors to the containers opened inward to reveal various scenes inspired by the shadow boxes of Joseph Cornell. Paul Simon played at that party, and a French troupe of firework specialists put on a show. My wife, Helen, and I still host these parties every couple of years as an excuse to reacquaint everybody, and the guest list continues to grow.

Another thing about the parties—I didn't want people walking around competing with each other about which great designer they were wearing. The whole idea of creating that kind of dress-for-success stress was anathema to me, but I knew that's what would happen. So I leveled the playing field by making the invitations—and the tickets to get in—T-shirts. Guests, no matter who they are, cannot be admitted to the party without wearing their shirts in some shape or form. People make their shirts into ties and hats and skirts and scarves. Randomly—and perfectly—the dress competition I strove to avoid evolved into a creativity competition on how to "wear" the shirts.

You can't imagine the pleasure I get walking into the venue and finding eight hundred people dressed in varying expressions of the same T-shirt. It's delightful, and it creates instant camaraderie and conversation starters. There's also a level of intellectual challenge, because the T-shirts are themed and accompanied with a puzzle, the answer to which is the name of the entertainment that year.

I view the people who work at EGI as family. And for the most part, they view each other that way. Maybe the more accurate word is "tribe." From receptionist to CEO, we impress on everyone the key cultural standards of our organization. We want them to understand the mutual responsibility that we undertake and the loyalty and trust we share. "The enemy is without" once someone joins EGI. In the end, it's my family office.

And just like with my family, I want everyone to be happy—to love what they're doing—and I'll go the extra mile to make that happen. One of my senior executives came into my office a couple of years ago and said she was thinking about leaving the firm after twenty years. She wanted to go to divinity school. "Why wouldn't we try part time?" I asked. "If this is where your passion lies, go do it. If it doesn't work out, it doesn't work out."

The way I saw it, she was valuable to me, both professionally and personally, and I wanted her to be happy. She recently graduated from divinity school, and she's still one of my top people. She's happy. I'm happy. And in this business, you never know when a divinity school perspective might come in handy.

CHAPTER ELEVEN

Making a Difference

Being an entrepreneur is not just about what you *do*, it's about how you *think*. It's about how you perceive the world. Entrepreneurs are the ones who are always looking for opportunities to do things better. They don't just recognize problems; they see solutions. They're always coming up with new ideas, and they aren't afraid to try them. They are the self-starters, the risk-takers, those who take the initiative. They are always thinking, "I can do that better . . . I can fix that." There is a perennial questioning. In my firm, everyone is expected to be an entrepreneur.

I have always had this mind-set, and I largely credit my immigrant-influenced upbringing for it. The United States was built by entrepreneurs who were largely immigrants. By nature, the immigrants who came here were self-selective. They chose to take the enormous risk of leaving their homelands and everything they knew for the unknown. For an idea. They came here and started businesses and innovated. They were a primary engine behind creating a world power.

Today, the term "entrepreneur" has almost become synonymous with tech start-ups, but that's a narrow definition in my view. I believe you can find entrepreneurs in every endeavor. It could be a start-up, but it could just as easily be within a conglomerate, in business, in academia, in medicine, in nonprofit, whatever. An entrepreneur is anyone who is independent, creative, inventive, and willing to take risks.

Entrepreneurs are *driven*. We are constantly putting a stake out in front of ourselves. What's the motivation? Well, I doubt that many company founders who reach billion-dollar valuations are motivated solely, or even primarily, by money. To be sure, making a lot of money is a carrot. But I would venture that most great entrepreneurs simply love what they do—whether it's problem-solving, building something from the ground up, or a passion for their product or service.

And great entrepreneurs are always great salespeople. Arthur Miller did the world a disservice when he gave us Willy Loman in *Death of a Salesman*. His vilification of the salesman as a shady, desperate person living a dreary, hopeless life was the exact opposite of what I've found to be true. Not only do I and the leaders in my companies have to represent our ideas to the external world, but we have to be able to sell our ideas to our own people. We need to galvanize them—in good times and bad. Without their buy-in, we won't succeed. It's the only way.

I'm often asked, "Can entrepreneurship be taught or is it innate?" My answer is that I believe there is an inherent entrepreneurial gene, albeit it's stronger in some than others. Education can help students identify, grow, and apply their entrepreneurial tendencies.

I am heavily invested in entrepreneurial education. It is at the center of my philanthropic efforts because I believe it makes a difference. Successful entrepreneurs lift all boats by generating jobs, innovating, and contributing to the GDP. They are the epicenter of growth.

I started promoting entrepreneurial education in the late 1970s. As University of Michigan alumni, Bob Lurie and I stayed involved with the school and had an ongoing dialogue with Gil Whitaker, Jr., then dean of the business school. In reviewing the school's courses and direction, it dawned on me that there was a huge gap in programming. U-M's business school—just like the others at the time—was overlooking entrepreneurship. They were teaching by rote formulas. But the right answer is not always found in a number or formula.

I illustrated this concept during a speech at Harvard Business School in 1988 by sharing a story with the students:

Abe and Sarah were a sixty-year-old couple who had been married almost forty years. They went on separate vacations one year and sent each other postcards. Abe wrote:

Dear Sarah,

The weather's great, and I'm having fun. I was sitting by the pool this morning and I met this beautiful 20-year-old woman. We swam; we had lunch and we talked; and tonight she's coming to my room for a candlelight dinner. I may get lucky.

I hope you're having a great time too.

Love, Abe

Sarah responded:

> Dear Abe,
>
> The weather is great here too, and I am also having fun. I was sitting by the pool this morning as well, and I met a handsome 20-year-old man. We swam; we had lunch; we talked; and he is coming to my room tonight for a candlelight dinner. I too may get lucky.
>
> > Love, Sarah
> >
> > P.S. Don't forget that 20 goes into 60 a lot more than 60 goes into 20.

You see? It's not what the numbers are that matters. It's what they *mean*.

After I finished speaking, the students came up as usual for side conversations. The fifth one was a guy who walked up and asked, "Where's the shrimp?" Huh? I said, "Excuse me?" And he replied, "Where's the buffet? You're here to recruit us, right?" Apparently, even the guest lectures had become rote.

Critical thinking is the hallmark of an entrepreneur. That open-minded ability to independently assess is in direct contrast to a formulaic approach. Instead of fostering critical thinking, business schools were creating automatons. It was a huge waste of intellectual talent. Entrepreneurship was dismissed out of hand, labeled "junk science," because people did not understand what it was. Bob and I wanted to change that.

We began having conversations with Gil about what steps we might take to add the subject to the school's curriculum. Ultimately we decided that Bob and I would sponsor a national contest inviting any academic in any field to write a syllabus for a course on entrepreneurship. The winner would receive $25,000 and a one-year appointment at U-M to teach their class. Between 1981 and 1986, we had six winners—an eclectic and often surprising mix. The first was a music teacher, another taught English in prisons, and the most memorable was a professor of engineering from the University of Houston. His course was called "Failure 101," and it was based on the premise that to be successful, entrepreneurs needed to suffer, understand, and get very comfortable with rejection. For the final exam, he gave each student ten Popsicle sticks and told them to build something using the sticks. He then told them to go out into the quad (student center) and sell their creations for no less than $10 each.

You can imagine the comments and ridicule they received from other students. Of course, no one in the class made a sale. Afterward, the professor used the experience to teach about failure and how you come back from it. It was a great class.

Then in 1996, U-M called me to say an alum who had passed away had left a bequest for someone to run a one-semester course for undergrad honor students. The subject was up to the teacher, and the university invited me to teach a course of my own creation. I chose risk because understanding and managing risk is so central to entrepreneurship. I asked the university to give me a Noah's Ark class—twenty kids from about fifteen different disciplines. My goal was to educate them on risk, not just in terms of finance, but in the construct of decision making. In the last class I began by presenting them with a challenge:

"Aunt Minnie has died and left each of you $100,000. You have an investment choice to make. You can invest it all at 7 percent for five years, or you can invest it at 7.5 percent for ten years."

After they had time to reflect, they unanimously chose 7 percent for five years. When I asked them what risk they'd undertaken with this decision, they said, "None." Their justification was that by staying short, future inflation wouldn't erode their returns as much as the longer term, and they'd have optionality after the five years.

But they were missing the reinvestment risk. They were so focused on what would happen during the investment period, they neglected to look beyond the five years. Not a problem if rates stayed at 7 percent or higher. But if they dropped? Problem. Once the students understood there is risk by *omission* as well as by *commission*, my objective was accomplished.

Not long after that class, I felt it was time to establish something more permanent. I met with U-M's business school faculty and said, "I'm prepared to fund an entrepreneurship program if you put it together." They said, "Great. We'll get back to you."

I'm still waiting. That was twenty years ago.

The fact that I never got that call from U-M made me realize that to make a meaningful impact, a philanthropic program—just like an investment—needs an *owner*. Someone who has a vision, is paying attention, asking tough questions, challenging, and pushing for more results. That's why I've always hesitated to provide endowments. I prefer to structure gifts incrementally based on achieved metrics. As in business, it's about transparency, accountability, and setting people up to succeed. Anybody, if they've got the money, can just put their name on a building.

So in 1999, we took the initiative and established the Zell

Lurie Institute for Entrepreneurial Studies at U-M through the Zell and Lurie family foundations. The goal of the program is to help students recognize and develop their entrepreneurial tendencies. By design, the institute at U-M is both academic and application driven. We want students to learn how to think like entrepreneurs, no matter the setting, and then apply that learning to real-world challenges. An essential part of the program is hands-on learning—actually doing the work of entrepreneurial creation, and business competitions, which enables students to hone their thinking and get feedback from independent third parties in the community.

We also recently kicked off the $10 million Zell Founders Fund to help launch new student-led companies. Finally, the institute supports four other course-credit programs that help students learn how to be investors: the Zell Early Stage Fund, the Wolverine Venture Fund, the Social Venture Fund, and the Commercialization Fund.

I love interacting with the students, and I'm energized by introducing them to ideas they haven't considered before. I do about forty speaking engagements a year, and roughly half of them are at universities. At every one of those events, some kid will inevitably get up and ask the question: "You've done so much, but there is obviously less opportunity today. What are my options?" My answer is that there is *always* opportunity. It may not be broadcasting itself in the form of a sector-wide trend or a blatant disruption, but it's always there. You have to be actively looking for it, and when you find it you have to do the homework, assessing the risk versus reward. It takes guts, and it's not easy. But if you've got the stomach for it, it's a great ride.

Outside of U-M, I've started a few other entrepreneurship

programs through my family foundation—two at Northwestern's Kellogg School of Management and one at the Interdisciplinary Center (IDC) Herzliya, a private college in Israel. At Kellogg in 2001, I started the Zell Center for Risk Research, and then in 2013, also at Kellogg, we launched an incubator and accelerator program to help students create start-up companies. The premise of this program was fashioned after the curriculum at IDC in Israel because of its terrific success.

Here's how the Israel program came about. In 1994, I was invited to speak at IDC and I of course chose entrepreneurship as my topic. The founder of the university came up to me afterward and said, "This is such a great fit for our student body— maybe we could create a program." I was intrigued, and pledged my support. We developed an accelerator program that teaches students to apply entrepreneurial skills in the creation of real business ventures. The students are assigned to teams, and each team spends a year creating a company, living through everything that is involved from concept to launch. This immersion approach moves students beyond the theoretical and into the practical grit of creating a business.

The IDC program benefits from the fact that almost every one of the students has been through the Israeli military, so they tend to be older and more experienced in the real world than students in the States. They are already well versed in learning by doing. Most of them have firsthand knowledge of deprivation and extreme challenges in their lives, and they view this entrepreneurial experience as a staggering opportunity. They are passionately engaged, calling themselves "Zellots." It's not that the American students aren't motivated, but the Israeli students are really *hungry*. That's the key. In fact, when I interview new candidates for jobs, the first question I always ask them is "How hungry are you?" Hunger equals drive—an ever-present alertness that is always reaching, always stretching. It is priceless.

The IDC program, which began in 2001, is a landmark in entrepreneurship education. Fifteen years in, our three hundred alumni have generated over eighty registered companies in twelve countries—some founded by students and others by graduates. These new companies are diverse and imaginative. Most of the start-ups are tech-oriented, because Israel is geographically isolated. Alumni have raised over $400 million for their collective enterprises, which have been monetized through sales to companies like Google and eBay and through IPOs.

Some of the more memorable new companies started by Zell alumni include: Gogobot, a travel advice site; 24me, an award-winning next-generation personal assistant; Kano, a computer-coding kit for kids; and The Gifts Project, which enables users to give and receive group gifts on social networks and commerce sites. The latter sold to eBay. And there are so many more innovative and inspiring ideas these students have developed. The Israeli students represent much more than just global expansion or a mark on the map. I see great value and impact in shaping the next leaders of the "start-up nation." My favorite statistic about this program is that the companies founded by our alumni have so far created fifteen hundred jobs around the world, from Israel to New York, Beijing, Mumbai, and other cities.

One graduate described the program this way: "Take everything you need to know about being an entrepreneur, mix it with mentorship, add steroids, and you've got the Zell Entrepreneurship Program." We can't get a better review than that.

As an adjunct to the program, we created an alumni network. I knew that we could have exponential impact if we fostered the connections among students and committed alumni—essentially building a network of mentors. And in 2015, we broadened the IDC alumni network to include the entrepreneurship programs at all three universities. It's called ZGEN (Zell Global Entrepreneurship Network), and my vision is that, over time, it will become the equivalent of the Good Housekeeping Seal of Approval for employers and venture capitalists across the globe.

P hilanthropy isn't just an abstract concept for me. My parents taught me that you can never be truly successful unless you give to others. As I mentioned earlier, the concept of *tzedakah*, or charity, was drummed into me as a child. I'll never forget the way my parents took in refugees after the war, how they readily donated to Jewish causes, and how my father spent so much time helping people in his world with their problems.

I've been very fortunate, and that gives me the opportunity and personal obligation to have a positive impact on people's lives. If I were to talk about my legacy—and people ask me about that a lot—I would say that *tzedakah* is a big part of it.

My closest partner in this endeavor is my wife Helen. We had both been undergrads at the University of Michigan, but we didn't really get to know each other until I was at law school and I became friends with her husband. He and I used to play bridge together in the basement library between classes; one day I asked him if his wife played bridge and he said yes. When we all moved back to Chicago and had children, we did things together as families. But when Janet and I split up after twelve years, Helen and I lost touch and we didn't see each other again until 1995.

It was at a big art expo at Navy Pier—a packed room with

three thousand people, just the kind of mob scene I didn't enjoy. But my interest in art had been growing, so I escorted Ann Lurie, Bob's widow, to the event. I was walking around the room, looking at the collections, when I smashed headlong into a small woman, nearly knocking her over. I reached out to steady her, apologizing, and she said, "Sam!" I looked at her. "Helen?" We stared at each other in amazement. It had been twenty years.

We quickly caught up. Helen told me she'd been separated for a year and a half and her divorce was coming through in six weeks. I was divorced at the time, so I said, "I'm divorced; you're almost divorced. You want to have dinner?"

"Sure," she said. "Call me." And she walked away. After she left, I realized she hadn't given me her phone number, and her number was unlisted. But after a little sleuthing I found her and called her two weeks later. She came over for dinner and that was it. We became a couple pretty quickly after that.

It was serendipitous. Sharon and I had divorced the year prior, and I had just come through some of the hardest years of my life following Bob's death and the liquidity crisis in our business. Those events had forced me to rethink and reprioritize the value of balance in life. Also, at ages fifty-four and fifty-five, respectively, Helen and I both knew who we were and where we wanted to go. There was no need for pretense, no time wasted on silly stuff. We were completely compatible—we shared the same roots, had all the same references to culture and family. And most important, we shared the same values.

Helen slipped seamlessly into my world, and she thrived in the new experiences it provided. In particular, she brought a focus on philanthropy and the arts that I was missing but never had the time to follow up on. It was a unifying force that made us stronger as a team.

Helen has led our eleemosynary efforts to a whole new level. Our family foundation's work centers largely on education, the arts, and Jewish and medical causes—always with a special eye toward our home city, Chicago.

We've also gravitated toward early childhood development. An investor and mentor of mine named Irving Harris helped educate me on the importance of this issue. Irving was a very successful businessman who was passionate about the importance of starting kids off on the right foot. He created the Ounce of Prevention Fund in 1982 to support childhood intervention, from birth to five years. It was a public–private partnership, partially funded by government grants, but Irving put in most of the money. He was ahead of his time. When he started, few people were on board with spending money on early child care and education.

We've also honored my father and mother through early education opportunities with the Bernard Zell Anshe Emet Day School and the Rochelle Zell Jewish High School. My parents would be happy knowing that we further the Jewish teachings and culture that were so important to them.

While my primary passion is for entrepreneurship, Helen's is for arts and culture. She has also invested a lot of energy in building a program at our alma mater, the University of Michigan. The Helen Zell Writers' Program is a three-year, fully funded graduate program in creative writing leading to a master of fine arts degree. Like our entrepreneurial program in Israel, the writing program is an accelerator. It provides each student with the opportunity for a "Zellowship," a postgraduate year of financial support that enables writers to dedicate their time solely to writing, so their works can come to fruition. It has become one of the elite writing programs in America—a way of promoting the emergence of important writers. Our support for the Chicago Symphony Orchestra, the Museum of Contemporary Art, and the Chicago Public Education Fund also reflects our commitment to our home city.

Helen's passion for the arts is contagious, and she has helped me connect to it more deeply. I was surprised to discover I had an interest in art when I took art history as an elective my senior year of college. I found I could look at a painting and see stories and ideas that weren't necessarily the same as what everybody else saw. It was similar to the way I looked at business opportunities, but art tested the limits of my imagination in a whole different way. I was particularly drawn to the surrealists. I also saw art as a mirror of society. It reflected what was going on in the world and provided new perspectives on how those events were being interpreted. It is, in fact, a creative form of history.

So I was dabbling in art when in 1972 I got a call from a friend of mine, a lawyer who lived in London. He was representing Petersburg Press, one of the finest printers of lithographs in the world at the time. The press represented significant artists— Frank Stella, Jim Dine, and James Rosenquist, to name a few. But when the industry's business model changed to require printing up front, before printers got paid by the artists, the company ran into cash flow problems. So my friend asked if I'd be willing to create a credit line for Petersburg. I did, for ten years, until Petersburg became insolvent. I ended up with fifty pieces of art, security for the company's $400,000 outstanding loan from me. I had that art framed and hung in our offices. At first our employees didn't love it, but over time they got very possessive about their favorite pieces. So much so that when they'd move offices, we'd have to relocate the art in and around their offices accordingly. All of that art still hangs on our office walls today, and our conference rooms are named after the artists.

By the early 1990s, I had bought a few significant art pieces, but I wasn't focused on art beyond that. And then Helen came into my life, and she brought an enormous love of art and music. Together we decided to develop a meaningful art collection with an emphasis on the surrealist movement. Today people from all over the world come to view it. Watching Helen masterfully explain the interconnectivity of the works we've chosen is like going to school all over again.

When Bill Gates and others made their Giving Pledge public—a commitment to give the majority of their wealth to charity—I got a lot of calls asking if I was going to sign on. The idea of a public declaration made me uncomfortable, and I've always bristled at being pushed into a corner. Giving is a highly personal endeavor for me, as it was for my parents. It's like family—and you may have noticed, I don't disclose much about my family. But I do appreciate the sentiment expressed in those pledges, and I am also committed to using my resources to do good. I just don't feel compelled to tell people everything about the how, when, and where.

I'm often asked what I want my legacy to be. My best answer is "He made a difference." To do that, I have to test my limits every day. I have to influence events at the micro level so that they have a macro impact.

I've always been inspired by the words of Daniel H. Burnham, who was influential in persuading the Chicago city fathers not to build on the waterfront but rather to create perpetual parks along the lakefront and river—one of the most critical decisions that shaped my beloved city. He said, "Make no little plans; they have no magic to stir men's blood . . . Make big plans; aim high in hope and work."

CHAPTER TWELVE

Go for Greatness

For years I have had a minor investment in the Chicago Bulls, thanks to Bob Lurie. I was at dinner one night in the mid-1990s with Phil Jackson, who was the Bulls coach at the time. We were talking about Michael Jordan and what a phenomenal athlete he was. And Phil said, "What really makes Michael phenomenal is that he makes everybody else better." I can't imagine higher praise.

I believe my purpose in life is to make a difference, and I define making a difference as driving growth. Whether it's mentoring a young executive, turning around a faltering business, establishing an incubator for new companies, or whatever, it's about progress, improvement, *forward momentum*.

The tool kit I use to achieve my end includes the gifts I've been given. There are people who can draw. There are people who can sing. And there are people who can dance. I can make money. I see opportunity and convert it into something tangible. The business of making money just comes naturally to me.

People are always curious about how I do it, but to me the

importance of "how" is not in the deals I do, it's in the way I do them. I approach business like I approach life. To that end, I'll leave you with a few of my key philosophies.

Be Ready to Pivot

I never hesitate to pursue a new endeavor just because I haven't done something similar before. I just use what I've learned that might cross over. I see myself as a frontline player, and that means being able to envision where demand is going to be, or where it won't be—not just in the next five years but in the next twenty or thirty years. It means spotting opportunity early on so you can have first-mover advantage. And it means not sticking to assumptions that limit your opportunity.

So I stay nimble, ready to pivot. I am industry agnostic. I move in and out of real estate, manufacturing, pharmaceuticals, logistics, energy, and a bunch of other industries. I am opportunistic. Sometimes I am a buyer, sometimes a seller. Sometimes I'm an equity investor, and sometimes I focus on debt. Often both. I never let my affinity for any one industry or my love of doing deals dictate my actions. When there is a flood of opportunity, I raise funds to take full advantage of it. When good deals are scarce, I become much more selective and primarily just use my own money.

The fact is, I am eclectic, and the fun of my life is being able to gain access in new arenas. To be on the move. If you're not moving forward, you're falling behind.

Keep It Simple

I stay true to the fundamental truths: the laws of supply and demand; liquidity equals value; limited competition; long-term relationships; and the others I've covered. They offer a framework through which I view potential opportunity. Understanding the implications of changing legislation led me to maximize the opportunities of NOL vehicles, REITs, and Jacor. My attention to demographics guided shifts in strategy at all of my Equity companies. The mantra "simplify risk" became so ingrained in me that today I can talk to fifty people a day on investment ideas, listen to their list of twenty issues, say "It's this one; focus on that," and send them off to keep going.

I love unraveling problems—from crossword puzzles to billion-dollar deals. Problem solving is my passion, whether the problem on the table is my own, a colleague's, a friend's, an employee's, or my grandchild's. Breaking the issues down to their barest elements, simplifying them. Finding that fulcrum.

It's something anyone can learn to do—just as I once did from Jay Pritzker. After that, experience makes the difference—doing it again and again until it becomes instinctive. Experience builds discipline and insight that sometimes allows you to see over the abyss before you step into thin air. It's being *risk aware.*

When I think about this perspective, I often find myself contemplating my father's way. By the time I knew him, he was very conservative and very risk averse. And yet before I was born, he had taken an extraordinary risk—with no real ability to foresee how things would turn out. There were times when he and my mother were escaping from Poland that it looked doubtful they would survive. That changes a person, and I don't think that vestige of fear ever fully leaves you. By the time he arrived in the United States, my father's orientation was to work hard and keep his head down, stay under the radar, and avoid any risk.

However, he created a son—me—who was part of a new generation. I learned from observing and listening to him, and that made me more attuned to risk. But I had not experienced war and anti-Semitism firsthand. I grew up in a world that seemed wide open and full of possibility. If my father had been raised in this country as I was, I don't think there's any question that he could have easily achieved what I achieved.

Keep Your Eyes (and Mind) Wide Open

Did you ever wonder how the Jews allowed the Nazis to come into Poland without taking action? I asked my father that when I was little, and I'll never forget what he said. The Jewish community in Poland at the time was extraordinarily myopic—it had little idea what was going on in the world. And it cost most of them the ultimate price. In contrast, my father's macro understanding of world events and the conviction to act saved the lives of my family.

I apply the same strategy on a much less life-and-death scale. I rely on a macro perspective to identify opportunities and make better decisions, both in my investment activity and in leading my portfolio companies. I am always questioning, always calculating the implications of broader events. How will worldwide depressed currencies affect capital flows and world trade? Does it create opportunity for international expansion among multinational companies? What real estate needs will they have? How can we get a first-mover advantage into new markets? And on and on. Luckily, I don't need much sleep.

If there's one consistent theme, it's that I'm always on the lookout for anomalies or disruptions in an industry, in a market, or in a particular company. Recognizing the psychology of market extremes can lead to attractive points of entry. Any event or pattern out of the ordinary is like a beacon telling me some interesting new opportunity may be emerging.

I've said it before and I'll underscore it here: I am a voracious consumer of information. I have honed my ability to digest a lot of information, sift out what's potentially relevant, retain it, and then recall it when it's useful. I read at least five newspapers every day, and five business magazines a week. I remember all of it, or at least everything relevant. I also like to read escapist fiction—mystery novels, spy thrillers—and I go through about one book a week. I usually remember nothing about them. Unless all of a sudden something becomes relevant.

On one occasion my motorcycle crew and I were on a trip to Chile. On our last day there was a torrential rainstorm in the forecast, so we didn't ride and left early. En route we realized we were going to get home at 3:00 a.m. and that didn't make any sense. So we started thinking about whether there was any place we could stop along the way. We were coming up short on options. And then I remembered a random detail from a spy novel I'd read years earlier, where the final scene was a shoot-out at a resort called Casa de Campo in the Dominican Republic. The book had mentioned that this private resort had its own international airport. So the pilot checked it out, and sure enough it was real. We got on the phone and made reservations. We took off, landed in the Dominican Republic for dinner, and spent a wonderful day there. You can't predict when or how you'll learn something. You've just got to keep your eyes and mind open.

It's also about simply paying attention to people. Being a

good listener can make all the difference. Very early in my career, when I was investing in properties in Ann Arbor, we were on the verge of signing a deal with a woman to sell her home. We were planning to tear it down and build an apartment building. The owner started to renege at the last minute, and I couldn't figure out why. In every respect it was a great opportunity for her. I spent a lot of time talking to her, and the truth finally came out. She told me that her dog was buried in the backyard, and she just couldn't stand the idea of a big apartment building sitting on top of her dog.

That new knowledge made the difference, and I would have never accessed it if I hadn't kept digging (no pun intended). I immediately saw that there was a simple solution to what had seemed an intractable problem. I added a clause to the contract stipulating that I would give her enough time before knocking down the house that she could have her dog exhumed and buried elsewhere. And that's what happened.

The truth is, you never know when opportunity is going to present itself, and you might miss it if you're not paying attention. In 1988, when Itel acquired Henley Group, the CEO Paul Montrone invited me to Wolfeboro, New Hampshire, for a weekend of bocce. Not knowing anything about the game, I figured why not? How hard could it be to throw a ball? As I've said before, I suffer from being very competitive, and that is not limited to things I can do well. For the next twenty years I participated in Paul's world-class (kind of) event surrounded by a collection of extraordinary individuals. My opponents over the years have included Tom Menino, former mayor of Boston; the late Justice Antonin Scalia; Paul Plishka of the Metropolitan Opera; and many others.

Recalling my father's admonition that having fun was frivolous, I think I always set out to prove him wrong. In one instance, I took advantage of the fact that one of the guests was Alan Leventhal, CEO of Beacon Properties. Beacon was a newly equitized REIT focused on office buildings in Boston. In between yelling with the bocce referees (who were all biased, I might add), Alan and I started talking about Equity Office acquiring Beacon. The encounter resulted in a transaction that was completed in 1997 for $4 billion.

If you're a seeker of information and a serious observer, it's all there to be learned. But with today's access to an overwhelming amount of information, most of it drivel, you have to focus on what's meaningful.

Be the Lead Dog

"If you ain't the lead dog, the scenery never changes." The origin of this quote was humorist Robert Benchley. I've always loved it because it defines my basic approach. In my businesses, I like to be the lead dog, to control the "scenery" in every industry I enter. It means not being less than number two in any industry, and preferably being number one. If you're not the lead dog, you spend your whole life responding to others.

This mentality is on display in my companies. Equity Life-Style Properties is the biggest operator of manufactured homes and RV parks. Equity Residential is the country's leading owner of apartment buildings. Until we sold it, Equity Office Properties had the largest portfolio of Class A office properties. Covanta is one of the country's largest waste-to-energy companies. Sealy Corporation was the largest bedding manufacturer in North

America. Revco was the second-largest U.S. drugstore chain after Rite Aid.

One of my favorite lead dog investment stories is Adams Respiratory. In 1999, we got involved in Adams, a small pharmaceutical company with an ingenious strategy. When the Federal Food, Drug, and Cosmetic Act was passed in 1938, expanding the FDA's authority, existing drugs were grandfathered. If someone could prove they could make one of those drugs significantly more effective, they would get a monopoly on that improvement. Adams had developed a new slow-release, long-acting version of the grandfathered respiratory expectorant guaifenesin. So the plan was to successfully complete trials and prove the efficacy of Adams's clinical formula. If Adams was successful, it would significantly limit competition among makers of guaifenesin. And that's just what happened.

After the FDA approved Adams's drug in 2002, the feds sent warning letters to all manufacturers and distributors of long-acting guaifenesin, telling them to withdraw their products from the market until they had gone through the FDA's review process. This, of course, gave us a huge first-mover advantage in the market, and created significant barriers to entry for other competitors. Simultaneously, we launched a massive marketing campaign to introduce Mucinex—Adams's product—to the public. It worked, and Mucinex sales took off. Adams grew from $14 million in sales in 2003 to $332 million in sales in 2007. We took it public in 2005. In 2007, Adams was sold to Reckitt Benckiser for $2.3 billion. We realized $380 million in proceeds from our initial investment of $26 million, nearly 15 times our investment.

Let me add that being the lead dog is not just a business

strategy. It's a mind-set. And I think that mind-set is uniquely American.

America is the great equalizer. You can come from nothing, you can come with no pedigree, you can be the son or daughter of immigrants, and you have the opportunity to be successful. There's no other country that doesn't require some kind of birth heritage, or inheritance, or ingrown advantage. Here, everybody has a shot at being the lead dog.

Do the Right Thing

When you're in it for the distance, you do it right. Ethics are a cornerstone. One of my oldest and closest friends, Willie Weinstein, teaches business ethics at a university. We talk at least twice a day, and I often run ideas and deals by him to get his take. I look to him to challenge me and let me know if he can think of any ethical complication. Willie never hesitates to tell me exactly what he thinks, and I value the check and balance. We argue about a lot of things, but never about ethics.

I have always known that success for me would be guided by principles. For that reason, there are some deals I just won't do. For example, at one point in the mid-1990s, a bank officer called to say they'd come across a very interesting business. The bank wouldn't invest in it, but he thought I might take a look. It was a concept called payday loans—short-term, high-interest loans that would tide a person over until payday. I went to New York and listened to the pitch. From a risk–reward point of view, it was an extraordinary idea, because it filled a need for the borrower while producing huge returns for the lender. But after listening,

I finally said, "It's a fine business model, and probably very profitable, but I can't put my name on this. I can't be in the payday lending business. I can't charge a laborer 300 percent to borrow money for two weeks and live with myself. It doesn't matter if it's a good deal. It's not the business I'm in."

I look for that same sense of decency in the people I partner with. As the idiom goes, "If you lie down with dogs, you'll wake up with fleas." I remember some years ago, we were offered the opportunity to buy an interest in a mall. I was warned going in that the guy who owned it was really difficult. When I walked in and sat down to meet with him, the first words out of his mouth were "I just want to tell you up front, nobody has ever wanted to do a second deal with me." I almost laughed it was so classic. As the saying goes, when people show you who they are, believe them.

If I had to describe myself it would be 180 degrees from that. Everything I do is predicated on the assumption that there's another deal. And the way you get to the next deal is to play it straight. I know there's an attitude that you can't be both successful and ethical. I beg to differ. That's the underachiever's perspective on the world—it's the person who looks up and says, "The only way that that guy could have been that successful is by cutting corners or because he's a crook." Underachievers have been pushing that idea since the beginning of time. I don't buy it.

In the late 1980s, I was asked to recapitalize and reorganize Apex Oil, a St. Louis company that sold gas through its Clark retail stations, owned a couple of refineries, and had a significant oil trading operation. With the fall of oil prices at the time, Apex had gotten upside-down on its borrowings. In fact it was a big, complex mess, but I saw potential and agreed to put up $20 million.

The transaction was arduous, and it took the better part of six months. At one point, right before the closing, a rumor started making the rounds that I was going to walk away from the deal. As a result, the banks became very nervous. Deals have blown up over far less. That particular weekend I happened to be on a motorcycle trip in Wisconsin, which was home to a large number of Apex's Clark stations. During the first stop we made that Friday morning I got the call that the banks were getting skittish. I knew I had to convince them I was in the deal to stay.

The following Tuesday we had a bankers' meeting back in Chicago at the Knickerbocker Hotel. Everyone in the room was a little tense. I started the meeting by asking Sheli Rosenberg to pass out sealed, plain manila envelopes to all thirty participants. I told them not to open their envelopes until after I had made some opening remarks, whereupon I addressed the rumor that I might be backing out of the deal. I assured them unequivocally that my participation would continue until we reached a resolution. Then I asked them to open the envelopes. In each one there was an 8 x 10 photo of me in my motorcycle leathers striking a John Travolta pose in front of an enormous Clark station sign. Needless to say, it broke the tension. "In case anyone questions my commitment, this should set them straight," I said.

When I negotiate, I spend a lot of time thinking about the person across the table, their motivation and priorities. I work to understand which issues are the deal breakers for them—which three of the twenty things we're discussing they really care about. And of course I'm crystal clear on the ones that are most important to me. That way we can both get what we want. It's a win-win—the best kind of deal.

On Wall Street I have a reputation for pricing things so the buyer wins. I don't squeeze out the last nickel. For example, in the late 1980s when I was offering convertible bonds for Itel, I found myself sitting in Merrill Lynch's New York office one day in front of a very humorless bank representative. He told me, "Merrill Lynch is prepared to buy $200 million of convertible bonds for a six and a half percent return."

"Fine," I said. "Let's make it six and three-quarters."

He stared at me, not comprehending. "What?"

"Make it six and three quarters," I repeated.

"But Mr. Zell," he said, "we can do the deal at six and a half."

I said, "I know that. But a quarter of a point means relatively nothing in this transaction for us, and it guarantees that every single buyer makes a profit the moment they buy the issue. And if everybody's a winner, they're gonna come back." I knew that every one of those buyers would then become a candidate to buy from me in the future.

My definition of "win" is not binary. It is not a zero-sum game. Negotiation that leads to a winner and a loser rarely leads to a successful transaction, or another one down the road.

That's how it's been throughout my business career. Sometimes my team argues with me—they can't believe we're leaving money on the table. But I want to create an environment where everyone wants to keep playing.

Shem Tov

My son-in-law once observed that my businesses and I are like a brand, and I'm always thinking about protecting the brand. That's an interesting way of looking at it. What he was basically saying is that in everything I do, I'm consistent, and I'm never tempted to do something that's at odds with my name. Do things go awry? You bet. But I never go into something sideways, and if it takes a wrong turn I do my best to correct it.

In business, people always want to know who you are—in other words, will you do what you say, will you make a reliable partner? I remember back in 1978, before I got out of the development business, a department store company that owned a site on Michigan Avenue was interested in building a Neiman Marcus there. They came to me and wondered if I'd be interested. One of the largest and most dominant developers at the time was a Canadian company called Cadillac Fairview. We met with the CEO and discussed the site and the opportunity.

When I was done speaking, the CEO looked at me and said, "If you're who you say you are, how come I never heard of you?"

I said, "Well, here are five names of major real estate–related players. Check me out."

That was on Wednesday. On Friday morning, I was sitting in my office at 7:00 and the phone rang. It was the CEO. He said, "I've got good news for you."

"Okay, what?" I asked.

"You are who you say you are."

I always smile when I think of that, because it's what it's all about. I am who I say I am.

Prize Loyalty

I believe loyalty defines your character. Do you stick with your friend, colleague, or partner when it's not easy? Do you consider their circumstances as much as you consider your own? The length and strength of my business relationships and the longevity of employee tenure across the Equity companies are among my proudest accomplishments. I have more than my fair share of critics, but nothing speaks more loudly to me than that.

I was always moved by how loyal Jay Pritzker was to me. I remember once in the early 1990s, I was in a bind with Itel. Basically, I'd bought the container business with cash plus stock with a four-year put. That meant if the stock wasn't at a certain price in four years, the seller, David Murdoch, could require us to buy them or he could sell the shares in the market and we would have to make up the difference.

Well, you may recall that was a particularly tough period in my life—professionally and personally. We had just lost Bob, there was a recession, the Feds destroyed the junk bond market, lending was frozen, we were getting shorted, and there were weeks when I worried if I'd have enough cash to pay my employees. Itel's stock was recovering, but the point is that in January 1991, I was well aware that I had a put coming from Murdoch on March 31 to the tune of $50 million. Murdoch called me in February and said, "I'm going to put it to you," and he made it clear that he wasn't going to give me any slack.

By March 1, I was wrestling with where I was going to get the $50 million. Things were tight; there was no way I could get a loan. Meanwhile, Murdoch was calling me every other day, saying I could either give him the $50 million or just let him sell his stock. Obviously I didn't want him to dump $50 million worth of stock on the market, but he was really putting the screws to me. Murdoch kept asking "Are you gonna give me cash, or are you gonna let me sell the stock?" And I kept saying "I don't know."

Finally, about March 15, just two weeks before the deadline, I went to see Jay and I said, "Jay, I need $50 million." I explained my situation to him.

And he said, "Fine." That was it—fine. Thirty minutes later I had the money. That was Jay. And I never forgot what it was like to be on the receiving end of that trust. I would have done anything for him.

As you can imagine, for someone in my position, loyalty and trust are priceless commodities. And they go both ways.

Obey the Eleventh Commandment

Don't take yourself too seriously. I have to restate it because so many people do. Ego and pride have their places, but when they are not self-regulated, they can be detrimental, if not debilitating. But for me the Eleventh Commandment implies something more. Simply put, it's being the first person to laugh at yourself. Being able to laugh at yourself has nothing to do with the size of your ego. If anything, you could argue that the fact that you are the subject of your own mirth is a reflection on how highly you value your ego.

To me, the Eleventh Commandment acknowledges that we're all human beings who inhabit the world and are given the gift of participating in the wonders around us—as long as we don't set ourselves apart from them. My personal office is comfortable, artistic, and reflective of who I am. It is not palatial. It does not tower over the city—it's on the *sixth* floor, not the *sixtieth*. But I do have an outdoor deck. It's a lush plant garden that apparently attracts every pigeon in the city. (I've tried squirt guns, but the pigeons were undeterred.) It's also home to two stately, well-fed ducks with their own heated pool, which I guess makes me a bit of a quirky billionaire.

About those ducks. Many years ago, I walked outside one

morning and found a mallard duck sitting on the deck. I'd never seen a duck on my deck before, and I thought it was strange. The next morning, the duck was still there, this time with three ducklings. Her ducklings had hatched overnight.

Everyone in the office was excited about our new duck family, and for the next couple of weeks there was a steady stream of visitors. Then one day the mother and two of the ducklings flew away, leaving behind the third duckling, who appeared to be the runt of the brood and had a bad leg. We named him Dewey. So, what to do? My EGI employees are a very creative group of people, and they're problem solvers. They like to figure things out. So one of them took the duckling to a vet, who referred us to an animal chiropractor. Dewey went through physical therapy. I am not kidding. We built him a heated pool on the deck and he lived there for about a year, and he healed. (We'd bring him inside when it got too cold.) Then mating season came, and Dewey flew away too.

I, along with my staff, missed him. Everyone liked having a duck around, but we didn't want to keep losing them. Then someone suggested, "How about the kind of ducks that don't fly?" So, we did the research—they're called rouens—and we eventually ended up with two stay-at-home ducks. They're large and noble, with beautiful blue-green necks. We of course named them Huey and Louie. We're now on our third generation of ducks. They are just part of the Equity family.

I've said before that I never close my office door. So what do I do when I need a private meeting? In good weather, I take my guests out onto the deck, and there, surrounded by Chicago skyscrapers and the ducks quacking, we conduct our business. I like it that way.

Go All In

The minute you acknowledge that a problem is insurmountable, you fail. If you just assume there is a way through to the other side, you'll usually find it, and you'll unleash your creativity to do so.

I equate this fundamental truth with an entrepreneurial mind-set. It's tenacity, optimism, drive, and conviction all rolled into one. It's commitment to get it done, see it through, make it work. In my world, I call that being an *owner.*

For me, that means investing time as well as money. It means giving whatever it is—a company or a project—space in my head. I constantly think about it, how to make it better and how to introduce it to new opportunities. All with the goal of making a difference, effecting a positive change.

That said, as a rule, I generally don't let sentimentality influence my business decisions. It's how I'm wired, but it's also something Bob and I discussed back when we were first starting out together. With one exception.

Bob was a rabid sports fan. Every opening day for the White Sox, he would blast the game throughout the office over the loudspeaker system. When the team won its seventh consecutive game at the start of the season one year, Bob ran like a crazy man through the office with this big sign that read "7-0!"

One day in 1981, Bob came into my office and said rather formally, "We need to have lunch today." Well, there was nothing unusual about that. We had lunch together nearly every day, usually at the 181 Restaurant, which was on the ground floor of our building. We loved gyros and they made the best. So we sat down to lunch and I asked, "What's the issue?"

"I want you to call your friend Jerry Reinsdorf and see if we can buy into the White Sox." At the time, Reinsdorf was putting together a limited partnership for his purchase of the team.

I said, "Fine. I'll call Jerry and see how little we can invest to have a piece of the deal."

"No" was Bob's response. "I want you to call Jerry and ask him how much it would cost to have a *voice*."

And that's what we did. Bob sat on the board of the White Sox and later the Bulls. He went to a lot of games. I remember when we took over Tribune, which still owned the Chicago Cubs in 2007, Jerry called me and said, "You know, if Lurie were still alive, you'd never be able to sell the Cubs." And he was right.

I loved the way Bob lit up when he talked about baseball. He would have been delirious when the Cubs won the World Series in 2016. That level of passion is always appealing to me. I feel the same way when my wife, Helen, talks about her philanthropic projects, particularly the writing program she endowed at the University of Michigan. For Helen, philanthropy is about much more than writing a check. It's about immersing herself in the life of the project.

Let me leave you with this. An owner is consumed with making the most out of what he already has. He's all in. An entrepreneur is always looking for new opportunity. He's always reaching.

I believe those truths apply to life as well as business. Think about it.

I've never pushed my kids to work for me. Unlike a patriarch who created a widget manufacturing company and wants it to be perpetuated by his son or daughter, I've never had any aspirations of immortality through my business. This was *my* dream; I won't impose it on someone else.

I tell my kids and grandkids, "Your responsibility is to maximize the skills you were given. But whatever you decide to do, *invest* everything you have in it—*excel*. What I've done is not the example I wanted to set; it's the *way* I've done it that I hope you emulate, through focus, effort, and commitment."

This isn't a dress rehearsal. I try to live full throttle. I believe I was put on this earth to make a difference, and to do that I have to test my limits. I look for ways to do that every day. After all, I think it was Confucius who said, "The definition of a schmuck is someone who's reached his goals." It's up to me to keep moving the end zone, and go for greatness.

ACKNOWLEDGMENTS

For at least the last twenty-five years, all kinds of people have suggested that I needed to write a book on how I got to this point and the lessons I learned along the way. *Am I Being Too Subtle?* is an attempt to achieve these objectives in a readable fashion that is both entertaining and memorable.

I'd like to thank my dedicated book team, including the folks at Penguin Random House's Portfolio group, and the many people who were helpful in sharing their ideas, recollections, and input during the process.

I wouldn't know how to even begin to enumerate all the extraordinary people who have contributed to these adventures. Those I depend on—to challenge, support, inspire, or make fun of me—know it. And their trust and loyalty humbles me.

So much of our evolution and where we are today is the result of a collection of exceptional people working together in alignment. I measure much of my success by their individual growth and achievements, and they make me very proud. That gratification extends beyond those who are currently part of our organization to the many "Equity family" alumni.